LET'S LEARN ABOUT...
THE OCEAN

Teacher's Guide

Personal, Social, and Emotional Development

K1

Pearson Education Limited
KAO Two, KAO Park, Harlow, Essex, CM17 9NA, England
and Associated Companies around the world.

© Pearson Education Limited 2020

The right of Angela Llanas, Libby Williams, Karina Sanghikian, Lisiane Ott Schulz, and Luciana Pinheiro, to be identified as authors of this Work has been asserted by them in accordance with the Copyright, Designs and Patents Act 1988.

All rights reserved; no part of this publication may be reproduced, stored in a retrieval system, or transmitted in any form or by any means, electronic, mechanical, photocopying, recording, or otherwise without the prior written permission of the Publishers.

First published 2020

ISBN: 978-1-292-33407-3

Set in Mundo Sans
Printed in China (SWTC/01)

Acknowledgements
The publishers and author(s) would like to thank the following people and institutions for their feedback and comments during the development of the material: Marcos Mendonça, Leandra Dias, Viviane Kirmeliene, Rhiannon Ball, Simara H. Dal'Alba, Mônica Bicalho and GB Editorial. The publishers would also like to thank all the teachers who contributed to the development of *Let's learn about...*: Adriano de Paula Souza, Aline Ramos Teixeira Santo, Aline Vitor Rodrigues Pina Pereira, Ana Paula Gomez Montero, Anna Flávia Feitosa Passos, Camila Jarola, Celiane Junker Silva, Edgar França Junior, Fabiana Reis Yoshio, Fernanda de Souza Thomaz, Luana da Silva, Michael Iacovino Luidvinavicius, Munique Dias de Melo, Priscila Rossatti Duval Ferreira Neves, Sandra Ferito, and schools that took part in Construindo Juntos.

Author Acknowledgements
Angela Llanas, Libby Williams, Karina Sanghikian, Lisiane Ott Schulz, Luciana Pinheiro

Image Credit(s):
Pearson Education Ltd: Olivia González 70; **Shutterstock.com:** A_Lesik 50, Aksinia Abiagam 22, 22, Aleksei Martynov 20, All-stock-photos 56, Andrey_Kuzmin 56, antoniodiaz 12, Asier Romero 22, Bachkova Natalia 50, Boris Medvedev 64, Chanawee Champakerdthapya 68, CKA 68, cristi180884 56, Darren Baker 14, DGLimages 40, Dmytro Surkov 52, Dragan Grkic 40, Drpixel 28, Dudarev Mikhail 50, effective stock photos 50, Emese 14, Eric Isselee 50, Erika Cross 8, ESB Professional 68, fizkes 8, Flashon Studio 64, FrameStockFootages 28, Gaidamashchuk 20, Galina Gutarin 12, HorenkO 12, India Picture 28, Iryna Afonina 20, 20, Ivonne Wierink 64, Jan Mlkvy 68, Kichigin 52, Lena Bukovsky 20, LightField Studios 28, Maks Narodenko 56, Malvales 20, Michael Kraus 64, Monkey Business Images 28, NeydtStock 68, Nicescene 64, NikolayTsyu 50, Oksana Kuzmina 40, Ole_CNX 40, 40, Pixel-Shot 46, Pressmaster 8, Ravennka 50, Rawpixel.com 46, Regreto 36, Robert Kneschke 68, Ronnachai Palas 46, Sand T Laovanichvit 68, ScofieldZa 68, SLP_London 64, Sofi photo 8, stockcreations 56, Suthiporn Hanchana 64, Tanya_mtv 64, Tatyana Dzemileva 36, Toey Toey 12, Tursk Aleksandra 28, Valentina Razumova 56, Vangert 50, Vladimir Nenezic 68, World of Vector 20, Yellow Cat 36, Yuliya Evstratenko 12, ZouZou 14

Illustration Acknowledgements
Illustrated by MRS Editorial and Filipe Laurentino

Cover illustration © Filipe Laurentino

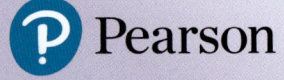

Contents

	Table of contents	4
	Presentation	6
U1	How are we all similar?	8
U2	How are we all different?	16
U3	What is a family?	24
U4	Do you share your toys?	32
U5	How do you help at home?	40
U6	How do you take care of your pet?	48
U7	What is your favorite food?	56
U8	What do you like about school?	64

Table of contents - Personal, Social, and Emotional Development

UNIT	LESSON 1	LESSON 2	LESSON 3	LESSON 4
Unit 1 How are we all similar? Page 8	• Use and respond to polite conventions • Know how to greet others • Accept and offer things politely	• Identify feelings • Express how they feel	• Identify feelings and what they represent • Name feelings	• Recognize that we all have feelings • Learn about the importance of sharing things with friends • Say thank you
Unit 2 How are we all different? Page 16	• Follow rules • Count up to three items	• Learn to play games with others • Follow rules and directions	• Review parts of the body • Understand and follow commands and rules • Learn to play together and respect rules	• Recognize oneself in the mirror • Identify differences between their face and their classmates' • Identify parts of the head and face
Unit 3 What is a family? Page 24	• Accept and follow rules • Learn how to be a good family member and a good friend • Understand the difference between good and bad behavior	• Identify family members • Talk about what they like and dislike • Learn to be a good friend and family member	• Compare different families • Learn to respect all families	• Accept and follow rules • Identify good and bad behavior
Unit 4 Do you share your toys? Page 32	• Identify and name toys • Learn through a story about the importance of sharing toys • Interact with others and share toys	• Talk about their favorite toys • Say which toys make them happy	• Review vocabulary related to toys and colors • Learn to share toys	• Learn to interact with others and respect other's turn • Use language to talk about being kind or unkind to others

UNIT	LESSON 1	LESSON 2	LESSON 3	LESSON 4
Unit 5 How do you help at home? Page 40	• Identify rooms in a house • Talk about their home and their chores	• Associate animals with their habitats • Understand that they need to take care of their pets	• Recognize when someone needs help • Name pets and ask questions about them	• Recognize when someone needs help • Distinguish between a doctor and a vet
Unit 6 How do you take care of your pet? Page 48	• Understand the sequence of a story • Learn how to take care of pets • Understand and follow commands	• Talk about healthy and unhealthy snacks • Talk about likes and dislikes	• Find out who needs help and how to help them • Dramatize stories	• Express likes and dislikes • Follow steps
Unit 7 What is your favorite food? Page 56	• Talk about food and say what they want • Talk about likes and dislikes	• Talk about food that is good for them • Take care of themselves and others	• Understand a story and talk about personal hygiene • Learn and practice vocabulary related to personal hygiene	• Talk about food they like and dislike • Talk about party food • Understand that people have different tastes
Unit 8 What do you like about school? Page 64	• Talk about what boys and girls like to play with • Understand that it is OK for boys and girls to play together with all kinds of toys • Talk about a favorite toy	• Learn about playing together and being a good classmate • Say where things are at school • Describe themselves	• Follow instructions in a game • Recognize written numbers up to nine • Count to ten	• Respect others and each other's turn • Identify and name playground equipment

Presentation

Let's learn about... is a bilingual program that aims to develop a wide variety of skills and subjects. To this end, several additional components ensure that students work on creative learning, pre-coding skills, STEAM lessons, personal, social, and emotional development, and much more. Teachers can find a complete mapping of the components online and suggested weekly planning to help them with their lessons in order to make the most of the cross-curricular proposal. All of the components of the program provide students with the opportunity to build a solid foundation and get ready for the challenges ahead.

As part of the **Let's learn about... Bilingual Program,** this component, called Personal, Social, and Emotional Development, aims to help students develop better interactions as well as a positive attitude toward learning and their school community. Moreover, the objective of Personal, Social, and Emotional Development is to provide students with the opportunity to grow personally and emotionally, learn to be part of a social group, and have healthier interactions with others, as well as contribute to their language development and general learning as part of the whole *Let's learn about... Bilingual Program*. Well-being and healthy relationships are closely connected to the following developmental skills:

- **Fostering positive relationships** – Learning to listen, being friends and classmates, sharing, and resolving conflicts
- **Building resilience** – Understanding that we all make mistakes, but we can learn from them
- **Collaborating** – Helping others and working in groups toward the same goals; participating and respecting everyone's turn
- **Feeling empathy** – Caring for others, understanding how others feel and that their actions may affect others
- **Talking about and expressing emotions** – Saying how they feel and understanding how others feel
- **Expressing likes and dislikes** – Saying how they feel about an object
- **Developing self-esteem** – Learning that they are an important part of the group and that they can accomplish their own goals

Learning to live with others

- Many young learners are skilled in their ability to cope with their own or other people's emotions in a way that creates positive social connections. However, some young learners might need extra assistance in order to become socially healthier. The Personal, Social, and Emotional Development program in *Let's learn about...* aims to help students acquire the ability to express their emotions correctly, interpret other people's emotions, and play or work with others.
- Having good physical, social, mental, and emotional health is essential to contributing to students' well-being. Personal, Social, and Emotional Development promotes activities to foster students' relationships and boost their self-esteem. Studies show that children with higher self-esteem benefit greatly from their social interactions, as they exhibit more social abilities and happiness as well as lower rates of aggression. Self-evaluations are also suggested because they help students become more autonomous, reflect on their progress, and leave "doubt" behind them.
- The program also has activities to increase self-awareness; thus, students will be more skilled at communicating and better at understanding others' feelings. Additionally, this component aims to help students learn in the early childhood stage to express their emotions in order to fit different social situations. For example, someone may feel angry at school, but they know that being aggressive is not appropriate in any social context. The program helps students reflect on how changing or controlling negative emotions in social situations is an important feature to help them fit in with different groups, create interpersonal relationships, and feel good about themselves..
- Empathy has been described as the ability to see from another person's perspective in order to understand what they are feeling. Empathy is an important component of the activities in this program; thus, the activities that help students engage in abstract thinking will help them to respond with empathy in certain situations. Talking about what they feel as well as what others feel helps students deal with intolerance and their own bad temper more successfully.
- Once students understand that they are working or playing together to reach the same goal, they are more likely to collaborate. This shows how important communicating with others is. When students have good relationships with their classmates, they learn that an activity works better when they take turns, share, follow preset rules, negotiate, and compromise. Students feel better about the group when they collaborate and have healthy social interactions, which also boosts their well-being.

What a Personal, Social, and Emotional Development lesson involves

As in any other **Let's learn about...** component, lessons in the Personal, Social, and Emotional Development Project Book propose the establishment of a routine for the beginning and end of a class, such as greeting their teacher, puppet, and classmates, talking about the schedule for the day, and saying goodbye.
The other activities that are part of a lesson aim to promote the awareness of the different ways people can relate to one another and how collaborating and having a nurturing and comfortable class environment can make learning more effective and enjoyable. This happens through the identification of feelings and situations represented in pictures or storytelling as a means to promote reflection on themselves and their interactions.

How to work with your Personal, Social, and Emotional Development Project Book

All **Let's learn about...** Project Books may have their pages removed. Before starting an activity in their Project Books, students can be instructed to take out the page they are going to work on and add it to a folder of their choice, so that students' work can be shared with parents regularly. This page, together with the projects students have developed in other project lessons, can become part of a portfolio created alongside with the teacher.
The aim of a portfolio is to show the cumulative efforts and progress students have made over time. This is also a great way to evaluate their improvement in all learning areas and the mastery of several skills. Students should be encouraged to share the work in their portfolio with their parents so that they can support their child's learning and be an active part of their development as a student.
An assessment chart is available in the Extra Resources folder at Pearson English Portal for teachers to print and fill out with students' performance.

Components

For students
- Personal, Social, and Emotional Development Project Book with pages that may be removed

For teachers
- Personal, Social, and Emotional Development Teacher's Guide
- Audio library with class content and songs available on the Pearson English Portal

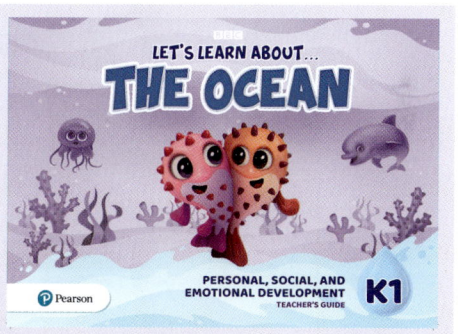
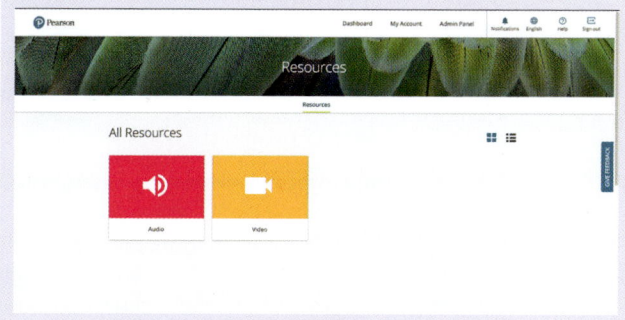

Presentation

Unit 1 How are we all similar?

CIRCLE THE CORRECT WORD.

HELLO.
GOODBYE.

HELLO.
GOODBYE.

PLEASE.
THANKS.

PLEASE.
THANKS.

PERSONAL, SOCIAL, AND EMOTIONAL DEVELOPMENT • HOW ARE WE ALL SIMILAR? • UNIT 1

Learning goals
- Use and respond to polite conventions
- Know how to greet others
- Accept and offer things politely

Main language content
Hello, goodbye, please, thanks.
Yes, please./No, thanks.
Feelings: *happy, sad*

OPENING

Circle time

Materials and preparation
- Feelings chart
- Puppet
- Visual schedule pictures

Have all the students sit in a circle, facing you. Say *hello* to them and encourage students to answer. Ask the puppet, *How are you today?* and make it answer by pointing to the Feelings chart. Ask students the same question and invite them to do the same as the puppet.
Show students the visual schedule pictures. Tell students the schedule for the day and have them point to the picture that represents each of the activities.

> **Note to teachers**
> Whenever you find necessary, use an attention-getter to have students focus on you.
> **T:** *All set?*
> **S:** *You bet!*

Play *Burst the balloon*.

Materials and preparation
- Balloons
- Pictures that convey the words *please, thank you, hello,* and *goodbye*
- String

Tell students you are going to play a game. Show them the filled up balloons and tell them each balloon has a picture inside. Explain that you will attach each balloon to a student's leg and they will have to try to burst one another's balloon. When they do so, they have to find the picture and mime what it does. Set up expectations of walking safely so as to avoid accidents.

Personal, Social, and Emotional Development

ACTIVE LEARNING

Magic bag

Materials and preparation

- A bag
- A book
- A crayon
- A pencil
- An apple
- Flashcards: *ant, cat, duck*

Prepare a bag with some items that students are familiar with from the unit (pencil, cat, apple, duck, book, etc.) Tell students you are going to play a game. Bring the magic bag forward and explain you have several items in your bag. Take out each item slowly and have students call out its name.

Now put all the items back into the bag and explain to students that you will be taking an item out each time. If the item is an animal they have to say, for example, *Hello, cat!* and *Goodbye, cat!* when you are putting it back inside the bag. If the item is a thing they have to call out the name. After they call out the name call on a student and ask, for example, *Book?* The student can answer *Yes, please.* and say *thanks.* when they take the item. Model this part of the activity with a student first.

Come in and say *hello*. Leave and say *goodbye*.

Materials and preparation

- Sheet or tablecloth

Make a pretend door inside the classroom by draping a sheet over a desk or putting two chairs back to back with some space between them. Have students enter from underneath the sheet saying *hello* or leaving saying *goodbye*.

Note to teachers

Since *hello* and *goodbye* are very simple words in most languages you could teach them in one more language (*ciao – arrivederci* for Italian, *bonjour – au revoir* for French, etc.). Your students will be very excited to know how to greet in more languages!

Circle the correct word.

Materials and preparation

- Project Book page 5

Help students open their Project Book to page 5. Read the words for them and invite them to repeat. Then explain that they will look at the picture and circle the correct word. Point to the first picture and ask, *Hello or goodbye?* As they answer, show them which word says *hello*. Repeat with the other pictures. Talk to students about the pictures and have them mime for their classmates to guess. *What word does each picture show?* Review the words *hello, goodbye, please,* and *thank you*.

Note to teachers

Although students at this age are unlikely to be able to recognize letters or read words, exposing them to written text is a great way to get them started in literacy development.

DIFFERENTIATED INSTRUCTION

BELOW LEVEL
Greetings

Ask students to go around the classroom and practice saying *hello* and *goodbye* to each other. Encourage them to use body language such as smiling and waving their hands.

ABOVE LEVEL
Being social

Have students offer each other items from around the classroom. Student A says *hello* and offers the item. Student B says *Yes, please.* or *No, thanks.* Encourage both to say *goodbye*.

CLOSING

On the phone.

Divide students into pairs and tell them they will pretend they are talking to each other on the phone. Model how we use our hand when we pretend to talk on the phone and say *hello*. Ask students to repeat the same movement with their hands. Now ask them to talk to each other on the phone saying *Hello, I'm (name). I'm happy (or other feeling). Goodbye.* Encourage students to use facial expressions to show how they feel. Students take turns role-playing.

**SPIN A PENCIL IN THE MIDDLE OF THE CIRCLE.
MIME THE EMOTIONS.**

THINK!
WHAT GAMES DO YOU LIKE TO PLAY?

PERSONAL, SOCIAL, AND EMOTIONAL DEVELOPMENT • HOW ARE WE ALL SIMILAR? • UNIT 1 7

Learning goals
- Identify feelings
- Express how they feel

Main language content
I'm happy. I'm scared.
What's the feeling? How do you feel? How are you today?
Feelings: *angry, happy, sad, scared*

OPENING

Circle time

Materials and preparation
- Puppet
- Visual schedule pictures

Have all the students sit in a circle, facing the teacher. Review the procedures for gathering in a circle. Say *hello* to them and invite them to greet you back.
Show students the visual schedule pictures. Tell them the schedule for the day and have them point to the picture that represents each of the activities.

> **Note to teachers**
> Make sure to review the attention-getters they have learned so far, and teach them new ones whenever you find appropriate: *All set? You bet!* and *Macaroni and cheese... S: Let's all freeze*

Match the cards.

Materials and preparation
- Feelings chart
- Prepare a set of emotion cards for the following feelings: *angry, happy, sad, scared* (two of each card, one card per student)

Tell students that they are going to play a game. First show them the Feelings chart and teach them the words for the feelings. Show your emotion cards and explain that there are two cards of each emotion. Mix them up and give one to each student. Ask students to go around and find the student with the card that matches theirs.
When students have found the matching cards ask them if the card in their hands shows how they feel today. Ask, *What's the feeling?* Go over the feelings on the cards.

10 Personal, Social, and Emotional Development

ACTIVE LEARNING

Imitate the feelings.

Materials and preparation

- Cards showing feelings from previous activity

Display the emotion cards and ask students to imitate the feelings on each card as a class or calling them out individually. For example, you say, *How do you feel?* and the students reply with the feeling on the card you are holding.

Spin and mime.

Materials and preparation

- Chalk or masking tape
- Emotion cards from previous activities
- Plastic bottle

Take students outside or make space in the classroom. Use chalk or tape to draw a large circle on the floor. Divide the circle into four sections and put an emotion card in each section. Ask a volunteer to model the activity with you while you explain.
Have students take turns spinning the bottle and miming the emotion the bottle points to. Ask students to say, for example, *I'm sad*.

DIFFERENTIATED INSTRUCTION

BELOW LEVEL
Spin a pencil in the middle of the circle. Mime the emotions.

Materials and preparation

- Pencils
- Project Book page 7

Help students open their Project Book to page 7. Explain that they will play the activity in pairs now. Have them spin a pencil and say the word for the feeling the pencil points to.

ABOVE LEVEL

Have students play the game the same way as described in *Below level*, but have them say full sentences instead of saying only the feelings, *I'm happy. I'm sad.*

CLOSING

Think! question

Ask students if they had fun while playing the spin game. Then ask the *Think!* question: *What games do you like to play?* If they use L1, you can rephrase their ideas in English.

Say how you feel today and say goodbye to your classmates.

Materials and preparation

- Cardboard paper
- Glue
- Markers
- Popsicle sticks
- Puppet

Cut out even-sized circles out of the cardboard paper and give markers to students to make faces that express the feelings you have talked about. Glue a popsicle stick on each and ask students, *How do you feel?* Students should use one of the popsicle faces to tell you how they feel. Then have students say *goodbye* to each other, to the puppet, and to you.

Learning Goals
- Identify feelings and what they represent
- Name feelings

Main Language Content
I'm (happy).
Does (the sun) make you feel happy or sad?
Feelings: *angry, happy, sad, sleepy*

OPENING

Circle time

Materials and preparation
- Calendar
- Puppet
- Visual schedule pictures

Greet students and encourage them to greet you and the puppet. Gather them in a circle and review the procedures for sitting in a circle, walking safely, and not running in the classroom.
Finally show students each of the stages they are going to go through that day by using the visual schedule pictures. Elicit the names of the stages and help them remember these names.

Play *Let's all freeze*.

Tell students that they are going to play a game. Say, *Macaroni and cheese*, and students respond, *Let's all freeze!* Explain that as they say, *Let's all freeze!*, they should all play statue and stand still. You can have them touch different parts of their face as they do so. Then divide students into two groups and name them Group 1 and Group 2. Group 1 says *Macaroni and cheese*, and group 2 answers, *Let's all freeze!* Change roles so that both groups say both parts of the attention-getter.

Note to teachers
Using attention-getters or chants to play games is a great way of showing students their meaning.

ACTIVE LEARNING

Feelings imitation

Materials and preparation
- Pictures of faces showing different feelings

Show students pictures of feelings: *sad, happy, angry, sleepy,* etc. As you show these pictures, students should mime the feelings they see in the pictures. Ask a volunteer to model the activity with you first. Make sure to say the feelings and have them repeat it as they role-play. Make sure to model this activity more than once as it might be challenging for some students.

Happy or sad?

Materials and preparation
- Circles made with construction paper (one per student)
- Crayons

Tell students to make a happy or a sad face. Have students draw a happy face on one side of a circle of construction paper and a sad face on the other side. Model by drawing these faces on the board. When you say, *I'm happy*, they should hold up the happy side. When you say, *I'm sad*, they hold up the sad side. Call on different students to play being the teacher and give instructions to the rest of the class.

Talk about the pictures. Then match.

Materials and preparation
- Crayons
- Project Book page 9

Help students open their Project Book to page 9. Ask who is happy and who is sad in both pictures. Hold your book up in front of the class. Make sure students are looking at the picture of the sunny day. Ask, *Does the sun make you feel happy or sad?* Tell students to take a crayon and give them time to match the pictures with the happy and the sad picture. Make sure to walk around the classroom monitoring and helping students.

DIFFERENTIATED INSTRUCTION

BELOW LEVEL
Show me your happy face.

Go around the class and ask students to show you different faces. Say, *Show me your happy face. Show me your angry face.* Help them by acting out the emotion as well. Have them say, *I'm (emotion)!* together with their expression. Then divide students into small groups and have them say and show a feeling for the others to identify it.

ABOVE LEVEL
Show me your angry face.

Go around the class and ask students to show you different faces. Say, *Show me your happy face. Show me your angry face.* Help them by acting out the emotion as well. Have them say, *I'm (emotion)!* together with their expression. After that divide students into small groups and have them tell their classmate how they are feeling using *I'm (sad)*. As they do this, their classmates will make the expression for that feeling.

Think! question

Ask the *Think!* question: *What do you do when you are happy/sad?* Elicit and accept all their answers.

CLOSING

Sing a song and say goodbye.

Materials and preparation
- Audio library - songs
- Poster with the song lyrics: *If you are happy and you know it*

Ask students with a very excited voice: *Are you happy?* Have them answer. Then say, *If you are happy, clap your hands.* Clap your own hands to teach them the meaning of the sentence. Explain to students that you will teach them a song called *If you are happy and you know it*. Sing the song first by modeling each movement: *happy, clap your hands, stomp your feet, shout Hurray, do all three*. Then sing the song again (track 07) and ask students to join you. Finally say *goodbye* to students and have them say *goodbye* to you and the puppet. You can also have them sing *goodbye* to you to the tune of the song: *If you are happy and you know it, say goodbye*.

Unit 1 13

TALK ABOUT THE PICTURES. CIRCLE THE THINGS THAT YOU SHARE WITH YOUR FRIENDS.

THINK!
HOW DO YOU FEEL WHEN YOU SHARE YOUR THINGS?

Learning goals
- Recognize that we all have feelings
- Learn about the importance of sharing things with friends
- Say thank you

Main language content
Here you are.
Thank you. You're welcome.
How are you feeling?
I'm happy!
Feelings: *happy, sad*
Items: *books, crayons, food, toys*

OPENING

Circle time

Materials and preparation
- Puppet
- Visual schedule pictures

Chant the song below as if you were rapping it. Use the puppet as well.
Hello, darling,
Hello, darling.
How are you?
How are you?
We are fine, thank you!
We are fine, thank you!
How are you?
Have students wave at you and the puppet as you rap it. Finally show them the visual schedule pictures. Ask a volunteer to be the class helper of the day and help you select the pictures that represent the activities as you say them.

Note to teachers
Songs and chants are very useful opening tools as they help promote a friendly and positive atmosphere.

ACTIVE LEARNING

Share your colors.

Materials and preparation

- A set of blue and red crayons per pair of students
- Sheets of paper (one per student)

Have students sit students in pairs. Give each student a sheet of paper and tell them to draw two crayons. Give each pair two crayons: a red and a blue one. Say, *one crayon is blue and one crayon is red.* Encourage them to share crayons and to wait for the color they want until their classmates have finished coloring. Walk around seeing that this is happening. Encourage students to have conversations like this when sharing:
S1: *Give me (blue, red), please!*
S2: *Here you are!*
S1: *Thank you.*
S2: *You're welcome.*

Talk about the pictures. Circle the things that you share with your friends.

Materials and preparation

- Crayons
- Project Book page 11

Help students open their Project Book to page 11. Have them look at the first picture and talk about it. Help them by asking questions such as *What are the children sharing?* (Elicit, *Colored pencils.*) *Are the children happy?*, etc. Do the same for the other three pictures.
Have the students circle the pictures of the things they share: *crayons, food, toys, books.* Also elicit from the students the magic word used to thank people who share things with them.

Think! question

Ask the *Think!* question: *How do you feel when you share your things?* Elicit and accept all their answers. Then, turn it around and ask how they feel when others share with them.

DIFFERENTIATED INSTRUCTION

BELOW LEVEL
Please or thank you?

Have students sit in a semicircle. Ask a volunteer to stand facing the others. This volunteer will say *please* and their classmates stand up. They will say *thank you* and their classmates sit down. Have them do this in a fast pace, changing between the words.

ABOVE LEVEL
Give me the blue crayon, please.

Materials and preparation

- Crayons

Divide students into small groups and have each group sit in a circle. Place all colors of crayons in the middle of the circle. Tell students to look at their classmate on the right and ask, *Give me the (blue) crayon, please.* Their classmate should take the crayon and give it to them, saying, *Here you are.* Remind them to say *Thank you!* Repeat until all students have had a chance to ask for and have had an item asked of them.

CLOSING

Read *An important first day* and say goodbye.

Materials and preparation

- Big Book Unit 1: *An important first day*
- Puppet

Tell students that they are going to see a story again. Open the Big Book and show the students the first two pages of the story in Unit 1. Elicit what they remember and ask them where Karla tries to hide. Show the students the last page and ask them to describe what is happening. Read the text. Elicit how Karla's friends help her and how they all feel at the end of the story.
Say *goodbye* to students and have them say *goodbye* to you and the puppet.

Unit 2 How are we all different?

Learning goals
- Follow rules
- Count up to three items

Main language content
*What's this? It's a pencil.
How many pencils?*
Numbers: *1-3*
School materials: *book, crayon, eraser, pencil, scissors*

OPENING

Circle time

Materials and preparation
- Puppet
- Visual schedule pictures

Have all the students sit in a circle, facing you. Review the procedures for gathering in a circle. Say *hello* to them and invite them to greet you back.
Show students the visual schedule pictures. Tell them the schedule for the day and have them point to the picture that represents each of the activities.

Match the pictures with the numbers.

Materials and preparation
- Board
- Flashcards: *numbers 1-3*
- Masking tape
- Pictures of one book, two pencils, and three crayons

Draw a big circle on the board and divide it into three sections. Fix the number flashcards onto the board, one in each section. Tell a student to come forward, show them one of the pictures, and ask, *How many (books)?* The student answers with the right number and you help them fix the picture in the right section using masking tape.
Hold up the pictures of the items and elicit their names, *What's this? It's a (crayon).* Ask students, *How many (pencils)?* and students answer with the number.

Personal, Social, and Emotional Development

ACTIVE LEARNING

Talk about the pictures.

Materials and preparation
- Project Book page 13

Help students open their Project Book to page 13. Ask what the children are doing. Elicit that they are playing with their toys. Then ask, *What kind of toys do you see? How many toys? How do they feel?*

Listen and stick.

Materials and preparation
- Audio library – class content
- Unit 2 stickers

Tell students that they are going to listen to a story about Mary, Sam, and their dad. Point to the pictures and ask, *Who is Mary? Who is Sam? Who is Dad?* Elicit their answers. Then play the audio (track 02) twice.

Audio script

Mary and Sam are playing with their toys. Dad tells them to put their toys away and come to dinner. Dad goes back to the living room and steps on one of the toys. Dad says, "I told you to put your toys away."

Ask students to think about the order of the pictures and help them go to the end of their Project Book to find the number stickers. Ask, *Which picture is number 1? Which picture is number 2? Which picture is number 3?* Students put the stickers in the right box following your instructions. Ask students, *How do the children feel in picture number 1? (Happy.) How do they feel in picture number 3? (Sad.)*

Sort out the blocks.

Materials and preparation
- Blue, red, and yellow building blocks
- Blue, red, and yellow mats or container

Ask students to sort the building blocks and place them on the mats/containers according to color. Have them count how many there are on each mat, *one, two, three*.

DIFFERENTIATED INSTRUCTION

BELOW LEVEL
Give instructions on how many building blocks of each color will go to each container or mat.

ABOVE LEVEL
Give students papers and pencils and give them instructions to draw *two crayons, three erasers*, etc.

CLOSING

Talk about putting toys away and draw. Then say goodbye.

Materials and preparation
- Paper
- Pencil

Ask students if they put their toys away. Give them paper and pencil and ask them to draw how their parents feel when they put their toys away (happy face, or sad face). Ask, *How do they feel?* Put all drawings in a visible place and point out how all the faces are happy when they follow the rules. When they finish, ask them to tell the class how their parents feel and then say *goodbye* to the whole class.

Learning goals

- Learn to play games with others
- Follow rules and directions

Main language content

Touch your toes. Bring leg. How many?
Parts of the body: *arm, finger, hand, leg, toe*
Numbers: *1-5*

OPENING

Circle time

Materials and preparation

- Puppet
- Visual schedule pictures

Have all the students sit in a circle, facing you. Review the procedures for gathering in a circle. Say *hello* to them and invite them to greet you back.
Hide the visual schedule pictures and have students look for them. When they find the pictures, tell them to bring them back to the circle. Tell them the schedule for the day and have them point to the picture that represents each of the activities.

Play *Hear it and bring an object.*

Materials and preparation

- Flashcards: *arm, fingers, hand, leg, toes*

Explain to students that you are going to play a game. Tell them that you have put up pictures of various parts of the body around the classroom and that you will call them out one by one. As soon as you call them out, they should go around, find the item and bring it to you. Say, for example, *Bring leg!*, and encourage students try to find the picture of the leg and bring it back to you. You should set up expectations of walking safely so as to avoid accidents.
When students have brought all the pictures back raise one flashcard at a time and elicit the names of the items portrayed.

ACTIVE LEARNING

Listen to your teacher. Play the game and stick.

Materials and preparation

- Boxes
- Circle cutouts (about ten per student)
- Unit 2 stickers - part 2

Help students open their Project Book to page 15. Hold up the page, point to each of the pictures and elicit the words from the students (*legs*, *arms*, *hands*, *foot*, *toes*, *fingers*). Help them go to the end of their Project Book to find the circles stickers. Ask them to count the legs in picture 1, the foot in picture 2, the fingers on the hand in the picture 3, the arms in picture 4, and the hands in picture 5. Help them stick the same amount of circle in the empty box next to it.

Ask students individually while pointing at the boxes in the page, *How many circles in this box, (Student's name)? How many circles in that box, (Student's name)?* Remind students to answer with the numbers.

Why is it important to follow rules?

Ask students to say how they played the game, the materials they used, how they decided how many circles to glue on the pictures, and if they could decide how many they wanted to glue. Then tell them that games have rules and ask them why it is important to follow the rules in a game. Make sure they understand that rules make the game fun and fair to everyone.

DIFFERENTIATED INSTRUCTION

BELOW LEVEL

Divide students into pairs and have them show each other the parts of the body while naming them.

ABOVE LEVEL

Write the numbers 1-5 on the board, draw parts of the body under each of the numbers, and elicit their names from the students. Have them also say what number is above each drawing.

CLOSING

Play *Simon says*.

Play the game *Simon says* calling out body parts. For example, *Simon says touch your toes.* and students have to touch their toes. The rule is that the ones who do the action without you saying *Simon says* are out of the game. If students are familiar with the game, allow a volunteer to take up your role and call out body parts.

Sing the *Goodbye song*.

Materials and preparation

- Audio library - songs

Sing the *Goodbye song* (track 05) with students. Encourage them to wave goodbye as they sing.

Learning goals
- Review parts of the body
- Understand and follow commands and rules
- Learn to play together and respect rules

Main language content
Boy, girl
Say the word. Count.
What is this? What are these?
This is a girl. These are legs.
Parts of the body: *arms, feet, hands, legs*
Numbers: *1-5*

OPENING

Circle time

Materials and preparation
- Puppet
- Visual schedule pictures

Say *hello* to students and have them say *hello* to you and the puppet. Gather students in a circle and review the procedures for sitting in a circle, walking safely, and not running in the classroom. Teach another attention-getter. Say, *Peanut butter* and students respond *jelly*. Explain that as they say *jelly*, they should all be quiet and looking at you.

> **Note to teachers**
> Constantly review the attention-getters they have learned so far. Ask them to mention their favorite one.

Organize students into small groups and give each group one of the visual schedule pictures. Say one of the moments of today's class and have those students holding that picture show it to the rest of the class and place it in the middle of the circle. Repeat until all pictures of today's class have been selected.

Wiggle it!

Tell students to take off their shoes and socks and sit in a circle with their legs straight out in front of them. Take off your shoes and socks and sit in the same position, close to them. Wiggle your fingers and say, *These are my fingers!* Wiggle your toes, point to them and say, *These are my toes.* Have students wiggle their fingers and toes.

> **Note to teachers**
> Make sure to set up clear expectations before starting any activity.

Personal, Social, and Emotional Development

ACTIVE LEARNING

Listen to your teacher. Play the game.

Materials and preparation
- Counters
- Project Book page 17

Help students open their Project Book to page 17. Give each student nine counters. Hold up your book, point to the pictures, and have students say the corresponding words or reteach them if necessary. Then call out the words. Allow students enough time to find the picture that corresponds to the word you said and place a counter on it.

> **Note to teachers**
> If you don't have counters, you can use buttons.

Sing Head, shoulders, knees, and toes.

Materials and preparation
- Audio library - songs

Sing the song Head, shoulders, knees, and toes (track 02) a couple of times. Then ask students to sing along and follow your gestures.

Sing and play.

Sing the song once again, but now changing the lyrics to different parts of the body they have learned so far. Ask students to help you choose the parts of the body to use in this song.

> **Note to teachers**
> Make sure to write the new lyrics on a flipchart or on the board as a reference, adding pictures to it. Students cannot read yet, but they will start to identify some letters and connect them to certain sounds if they can see the lyrics and pictures.

DIFFERENTIATED INSTRUCTION

BELOW LEVEL
Look and find.

Materials and preparation
- Project Book

Organize students into pairs. Have them look through their Project Book for different parts of the body and name them.

ABOVE LEVEL
Look and play the game.

Materials and preparation
- Project Book page 17

Organize students into groups of four. One student will call out the words and the rest will have to pay attention to place their counters on the correct pictures.

CLOSING

Count your fingers and say goodbye.

Have students stand with one hand behind their backs and the other up in front of them. Ask them to say the numbers. As they say them, they count the fingers on the hand in front of them, *one, two, three, four, five*.
Then ask them to change hands and count their fingers. Finally, ask students to clap their hands five times and say *goodbye* to you and the puppet.

OPENING

Circle time

Materials and preparation
- Puppet
- Visual schedule pictures

Have each of the students greet the puppet and have the puppet reply back.
Select the visual schedule pictures you will need and place them out of order on the board. Then say each class activity in the order it will happen and ask the students to point to it. Put the pictures in order as they point to the corresponding pictures.

Do it as I say.

Have students stand up and review the parts of the face by pointing to them and having the class say what part it is. Help them by saying the initial sound if necessary. Then give students some commands such as:
Open/Close your eyes/mouth.
Touch your ears/nose/hair.

> **Note to teachers**
> Praise students who can follow your commands. This will draw the others' attention and may give them time to copy these classmates' movements. Take care to praise the other students' effort as well.

Learning goals
- Recognize oneself in the mirror
- Identify differences between their face and their classmates'
- Identify parts of the head and face

Main language content
Are your eyes big or small?
How many eyes do you have?
Touch your (ears)!
Parts of the head: *ears, eyes, hair, mouth, nose*

Personal, Social, and Emotional Development

ACTIVE LEARNING

Match the boy's front with his back.

Materials and preparation
- Crayons
- Project Book page 19

Help students open their Project Book to page 19. Have them look at the picture of the boy. Elicit a description of the boy's face and features. If students do not mention this, call their attention to the boy's hair. Have them match the boy's front with his back. Ask them how they knew which one was the right one.

Listen. Draw your face.

Materials and preparation
- A few small hand mirrors
- Audio library - class content

Hand out a small mirror to a few students. Say *nose*. Have students look in the mirror, find their nose in the reflection, point to it and say, *My nose*. Continue with *mouth, eyes, ears*, and *hair*. Have students listen to the audio (track 03). As they listen, they should point to the parts of their face and then touch the ground and turn around. Then have students draw themselves. Monitor the activity and ask them about the parts of the face they are drawing. Ask, *Are your eyes big or small? How many eyes do you have?*

Audio script

Touch your ears!
Ears!
Touch your mouth!
Mouth!
Touch your eyes!
Eyes!
Touch your nose!
Nose!
Touch the ground
And turn around!

How are our faces different?

Materials and preparation
- Mirrors (one per pair of students or have them share)

Have students look at themselves in the mirror and then divide them into pairs. Ask them to talk about their classmate's face and head, saying what is the same and what is different. They can refer to the eye and hair color, or say if they both have big or small eyes. Monitor and help as needed.

DIFFERENTIATED INSTRUCTION

BELOW LEVEL
I like my eyes!

Materials and preparation
- Project Book page 19

Ask students to describe their drawing to a classmate, saying what they like best about their faces: *I like my eyes!*

ABOVE LEVEL
Mirror me.

Have students work in pairs. Tell them to face each other to mirror their movements. So, if one of them closes their eyes, the other one should do the same. Have them make faces and say the part of their face that is moving.

CLOSING

Play *What am I touching?* and sing the *Goodbye* song.

Materials and preparation
- Audio library - songs
- Puppet

Touch different parts of your head and face and elicit their names from students. Ask volunteers to touch the different parts of their heads and faces and have their classmates name them. Instead of eliciting the names of the parts of the head, you can say these names and have students touch these parts.
Wave goodbye to the students while singing the *Goodbye* song (track 05). Then have them say *goodbye* to you and the puppet.

Unit 3 What is a family?

ARE YOU A GOOD FAMILY MEMBER? COLOR THE RIGHT FACE.

ARE YOU A GOOD FRIEND? COLOR THE RIGHT FACE.

PERSONAL, SOCIAL, AND EMOTIONAL DEVELOPMENT • WHAT IS A FAMILY? • UNIT 3   21

Learning goals
- Accept and follow rules
- Learn how to be a good family member and a good friend
- Understand the difference between good and bad behavior

Main language content
Are you good? Are you bad? Do you listen?
I'm sad. I'm happy. My sister is well.
My daddy is great.
Adjectives: *bad, good, happy, sad*
Family: *brother, daddy, mommy, sister*

OPENING

Circle time

Materials and preparation
- Puppet
- Visual schedule pictures

Have all the students sit in a circle, facing you. Review the procedures for gathering in a circle. Say *hello* to them and invite them to greet you back.
Hide the visual schedule pictures and have students look for them. When they find the pictures, tell them to bring them back to the circle. Tell them the schedule for the day and have them point to the picture that represents each of the activities.

Saying positive things

Say the following to students while using your body language to help them understand. Observe their reactions while they are listening to you.
You are special to me.
I enjoy spending time with you.
Have a good day!
You are a good friend.
Ask students how they felt hearing this from you,
Did you feel sad or happy? Why? Was I good or bad to you?
Then tell students to say something positive about their family. Help them with the language.

Personal, Social, and Emotional Development

ACTIVE LEARNING

Are you a good family member? Color the right face.

Materials and preparation
- Crayons
- Project Book page 21

Help students open their Project Book to page 21 and have them take a look at the pictures. Ask, *What do you see? A boy, a girl, a daddy. Is daddy happy? Is the boy/girl happy? What is the boy doing? Playing/eating/sharing*, etc.

Draw students' attention to the happy and sad faces available. Ask, *What does each face show? Which one is the happy face? Which one is the sad face?*

Then ask students if they do these actions: *Do you play? Do you share toys? Do you listen to mommy/daddy? Are you good? Are you bad?*

Invite students to color the face (happy or sad) that shows if they are good or bad. Explain to them that listening, sharing, and being good are very important for family and friends. Repeat the activity with the other two pictures.

Make a good and bad behavior poster.

Materials and preparation
- Butcher or poster paper
- Glue
- Magazine cutouts of good or bad behavior
- Marker

Gather students around the butcher paper and show them the magazine cutouts you have brought. Tell them that you are going to categorize and glue these behaviors on the butcher paper. Divide the poster into two sections, one with a happy face and one with a sad face. Hold up a cutout, and ask, *Good or bad?* Allow students to glue the cutout in the appropriate section.

DIFFERENTIATED INSTRUCTION

BELOW LEVEL

In pairs, have students act out bad or good behavior and have their classmate say *good* for praise or *no* when the behavior is bad.

ABOVE LEVEL

Bring a student forward and ask them to act out a good or bad behavior. Have the rest of the class make a happy or a sad face depending on the behavior.

CLOSING

Sing the *Goodbye song*.

Materials and preparation
- Audio library - songs

Tell students they are going to listen to the *Goodbye song*. Play the audio (track 05) and pause after a while. Say one of the following sentences and have them repeat, *I'm a good friend! I'm a good family member!* Pause again and say the other sentence. Have them do so very enthusiastically. Say *goodbye* to students and have them say *goodbye* to you.

POINT TO THE FAMILY MEMBERS.

DRAW YOUR FAMILY MEMBERS.

PERSONAL, SOCIAL, AND EMOTIONAL DEVELOPMENT • WHAT IS A FAMILY? • UNIT 3 — 23

Learning goals
- Identify family members
- Talk about what they like and dislike
- Learn to be a good friend and family member

Main language content
This is my mommy. I like daddy. Who is it?
Family: *brother, daddy, mommy, sister*

OPENING

Who is it?

Materials and preparation
- Puppet
- Visual schedule pictures

Have all the students sit in a circle, facing you. Review the procedures for gathering in a circle. Say *hello* to them and invite them to greet you back.
Place the visual schedule pictures face down in the circle. Say the schedule for the day, one activity at a time, and have different students turn over the cards looking for the picture that represents the activity.

> **Note to teachers**
> When inviting students to activities in which only a few can participate, make sure to call different students each time and allow everyone to participate at some point.

Who is it?

Materials and preparation
- Flashcards: *brother, daddy, mommy, sister*

Bring out the family members flashcards. Hold up each card and elicit the family members' names from the students. Ask, *Who is it? It's mommy!*
Now tell students the next game is all about speed. The student who says the name of the family member first gets a point. Hold up a card facing toward you and flash it really fast for the students to see. Give a point to the first who identifies the family member.

Personal, Social, and Emotional Development

ACTIVE LEARNING

Point to the family members.

Materials and preparation
- Project Book page 23

Help students open their Project Book to page 23. Tell them that you are going to read something and they have to point to the picture of the family member mentioned. Read the following:
This is my mommy. She is very pretty. This is my daddy. His name is Bill. And this is my sister. She likes playing with her dolls. Oh, and this is me, my name is Sam.
Students point to the right picture while you are reading.

Draw your family members.

Materials and preparation
- Crayons
- Project Book page 23

Have students draw their family members in the frame. Go around the classroom and ask them questions, *Who is this? What's his name? How many people are there in your family?*

DIFFERENTIATED INSTRUCTION

BELOW LEVEL

While you are reading the script in *Active learning*, pause and give time for students to point to the right picture.

ABOVE LEVEL

Invite students to improvise and try to remember the script. They can say, *This is daddy, this is mommy, this is me*, etc.

CLOSING

Do a gallery walk. Say goodbye.

Materials and preparation
- Sticky tape

Hang all family pictures around the classroom and invite students to make observations about them, *Are all families the same? How are they different?*
Say *goodbye* to students one by one and have them say *goodbye* to you.

DRAW A STAR NEXT TO THE FAMILY THAT IS SIMILAR TO YOURS. SAY.

THINK! WHO DO YOU LIVE WITH?

PERSONAL, SOCIAL, AND EMOTIONAL DEVELOPMENT • WHAT IS A FAMILY? • UNIT 3   25

Learning goals
- Compare different families
- Learn to respect all families

Main language content
Big, small
Clap once, twice, three times!
Family: *brother, daddy/dad, mommy/mom, sister*

OPENING

Circle time

Materials and preparation
- Puppet
- Visual schedule pictures

Gather students and review the procedures for sitting in a circle, walking safely, and not running in the classroom. Say *hello* to them and have them say *hello* to you and the puppet. Make it say *hello* back to the students.
Then place the visual schedule pictures face down in the middle of the circle. Say one of the stages of today's class and call on students to turn over the pictures trying to find the one that represents that stage. Repeat until all correct pictures have been turned over.

Clapping pattern

Make a clapping pattern with students. Clap once. Students clap once. Clap twice. Students clap twice. Clap three times. Students clap three times. Clap four times. Students clap four times. Go back to clapping once and continue the pattern. After a while, students will join in the clapping pattern on their own.

> **Note to teachers**
> You can use this activity as an attention-getter, too. TPR (Total Physical Response) activities are also a great way of bringing students back when they lose focus.

Personal, Social, and Emotional Development

ACTIVE LEARNING

Think! question

Materials and preparation
- Project Book page 25

Help students open their Project Book to page 25 and encourage them to talk about the pictures. You might say, *Show me the big families, show me the small families.* Ask students the *Think!* question: *Who do you live with?* Elicit answers.

Draw a star next to the family that is similar to yours.

Materials and preparation
- Crayons
- Pictures of your family: prepare them in advance
- Project Book page 25

Talk about yourself. Show pictures of your family and say, for example, *I have a mom, a dad, and a brother.* Point to the picture of the family of four. Say, *Look! This family is similar to my family!* Then have students point to the family that is similar to theirs and draw a star next to it.

> **Note to teachers**
> Make sure to bring meaningful pictures of your family. Students start making connections once they see the real intention and meaning in your attitudes.

DIFFERENTIATED INSTRUCTION

BELOW LEVEL
Describe your family.

Organize students into pairs and have them share a description of their family with their classmates.

ABOVE LEVEL
Describe and compare families.

Materials and preparation
- Pictures of different families: prepare them in advance

Organize students into groups. Hand out pictures of different families and tell them to describe and compare the families in the pictures to their own families.

CLOSING

Sing *Big and small family* and say goodbye.

Materials and preparation
- Audio library - songs

Ask students to sit in a circle and have them listen to the *Big and small family* song (track 23).
As they hear the words *big* and *small*, ask students to jump twice. Make sure to ask them to repeat the words *big* and *small* as they hear them.
As you say *goodbye*, ask them to say what they liked most about today's class.

ARE YOU A GOOD FAMILY MEMBER? STICK THE CORRECT FACE.

ARE YOU A GOOD FRIEND? STICK THE CORRECT FACE.

  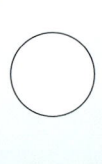

PERSONAL, SOCIAL, AND EMOTIONAL DEVELOPMENT • WHAT IS A FAMILY? • UNIT 3 27

Learning goals
- Accept and follow rules
- Identify good and bad behavior

Main language content
Are you a good friend?
Are you a good brother?
Yes. No.
Family: *brother, daddy, mommy, sister*
Adjectives: *bad, good, happy, sad*

OPENING

Circle time

Materials and preparation
- Puppet
- Visual schedule pictures

Greet students and have them sit in a circle, facing you. Review the procedures for gathering in a circle. Then teach students the attention-getter: *Hands on top, everybody stop!*
Show students the visual schedule pictures. Ask a volunteer to be the class helper of the day and help you select the pictures that represent the activities as you say them.

Are you a good friend?

Have students stand up. Tell them that you are going to ask a few questions and they should jump every time their answer is *yes*. Ask them questions such as, *Are you a good friend? Are you a bad friend? Are you a good family member? Are you happy? Are you sad?* As you ask the questions, help them understand the meaning of the sentences by miming *good, bad, friend, family*.

Personal, Social, and Emotional Development

ACTIVE LEARNING

Are you a good family member? Stick the correct face.

Materials and preparation
- Crayons
- Project Book page 27
- Unit 3 stickers

Ask students, *Are you good or bad with your family?* When students have answered, help them open their Project Book to page 27. Draw their attention to the pictures in the top half of the page. They have to consider the situations and decide whether they show good family behavior or bad family behavior. If the picture shows good family behavior, they should stick the happy face. If it shows bad family behavior, they should stick the sad face. Help them find Unit 3 stickers at the end of their Project Book. Check their answers orally.

Are you a good friend? Stick the correct face.

Materials and preparation
- Crayons
- Project Book page 27

Have students look at the *Are you a good friend?* situations at the bottom half of the page, and say which picture shows good behavior to friends and which picture shows bad behavior to friends. Then tell them to stick the happy or sad face accordingly.

Play *Good or bad?*

Divide the class into two groups. Choose students from each group to act out behaviors. The other students should react with a happy or sad/angry face according to the action the student makes. Encourage them to say *good* or *bad* as they make the faces.

DIFFERENTIATED INSTRUCTION

BELOW LEVEL
Point to good or bad.

Materials and preparation
- Project Book page 27

Have students look at the pictures again. Say *good* and have students point to the pictures showing good behavior. Then say *bad* and have students point to the pictures showing bad behavior. Have students work in pairs and continue the game, one of them saying *good* or *bad* and the other pointing. Have them change roles.

ABOVE LEVEL

Say some sentences to students. Mime the actions. Have students say *yes* or *no*. If the sentence is true, they have to say *yes*; if it is false, they need to say *no* and correct it by saying *It's good/bad.* Some sentences you can use:
It's good to play together.
It's good to fight.
It's bad to look after your little brother.
It's good to help.
It's bad to shout at your little sister.

CLOSING

Say the *Good and bad* rhyme and say goodbye.

Teach students the rhyme. Teach them one line at a time and your line, too, but focus on theirs. Then say the whole rhyme and have them say their lines.
S: *Be good, be good.*
T: *You really should.*
S: *Don't be bad. Don't be bad.*
T: *You'll make me sad.*
Then say *goodbye* to students and have them say *goodbye* to you.

> **Note to teachers**
> When teaching rhymes, chants, songs, and poems, it is essential to say the lines and mime. Exaggeration is welcome as well as making gestures to show the meaning of words.

Unit 4 Do you share your toys?

LOOK. ORDER THE STORY.

PERSONAL, SOCIAL, AND EMOTIONAL DEVELOPMENT • DO YOU SHARE YOUR TOYS? • UNIT 4

Learning goals
- Identify and name toys
- Learn through a story about the importance of sharing toys
- Interact with others and share toys

Main language content
The doll is big. The train is little.
Adjectives: *big, kind, little, unkind*
Toys: *ball, car, doll, plane, teddy bear, train*
Numbers: *1-5*

OPENING

Circle time

Materials and preparation
- Puppet
- Visual schedule pictures

Have all the students sit in a circle, facing you. Review the procedures for gathering in a circle. Say *hello* to them and invite them to greet you back.
Hide the visual schedule pictures and have students look for them. When they find the pictures, tell them to bring them back to the circle. Tell them the schedule for the day and have them point to the picture that represents each of the activities.

> **Note to teachers**
> Make sure to review the attention-getters they have learned so far, *Listen, carefully*. and *All set? You bet!*

Toys

Materials and preparation
- Flashcards: *numbers 1-5*
- Realia: a ball, a doll, a plane, a teddy bear, a train (you can substitute these with others that you may have handy)

Put the toys in front of students and ask them to count with you, *One, two, three, four, five*. Then call a student and say for example *Number one, doll*. and the student places number 1 in front of the doll. *Number two, train*. and student places number 2 in front of the train, etc.
Have students divide the toys into *big* and *little*.

Personal, Social, and Emotional Development

ACTIVE LEARNING

Look. Order the story.

Materials and preparation

- Project Book page 29

Help students open their Project Book to page 29 and ask them to look at the pictures. Say *doll* and ask them to point to the doll in the picture. Do the same with the rest of the toys and colors in the pictures.

Ask students to put them in the right order by drawing a line between them, from the first to the second picture, from the second to the third picture, and from the third to the fourth picture: 1) the boys are playing and a girl arrives. 2) the girl asks to play and they say no. 3) another boy arrives with his car and invites the girl to play 4) the boy with the car and the girl leave happy.

Talk to students about what is happening in the pictures. *Are all the children playing together? What about you? Are they sharing toys?* Make sure students realize that this is not happening. Then ask, *Is this kind? What about you? Are you kind?*

Ask students to circle the happy faces in the story. *Why are they happy? Do you share your toys?*

Make a kindness jar.

Materials and preparation

- A jar with a lid
- Hot glue (teacher use only)
- Pompoms
- Small items to decorate the lid

Explain to students that you are going to make a kindness jar. A kindness jar is a jar into which they will add a pompom every time someone does something kind inside the classroom.

Invite students to decorate the lid, but leave the jar transparent so that everyone can see what it has inside. Encourage them to put a pompom inside (with your help) every time they witness kindness. Ask students how fast they think the jar will be full.

This activity will help students visualize kindness inside the classroom as the jar will start filling up.

> **Note to teachers**
> If time allows, you can also have students make an unkindness jar and glue a sad face on it. This way they can see which jar fills up faster.

DIFFERENTIATED INSTRUCTION

BELOW LEVEL

Materials and preparation

- Project Book page 29

Say what is happening in each picture and have students point to them.

ABOVE LEVEL

Have students retell what is happening in the pictures.

CLOSING

Act out the story.

Divide students into groups and have them act out the story from *Active learning* in front of their classmates.

Sing the *Goodbye song*.

Materials and preparation

- Audio library - songs

Sing the *Goodbye song* (track 05) with students while waving goodbye.

CIRCLE THE TOYS YOU LIKE TO PLAY WITH.

COUNT THE TOYS YOU LIKE TO PLAY WITH. CIRCLE THE NUMBER.

PERSONAL, SOCIAL, AND EMOTIONAL DEVELOPMENT • DO YOU SHARE YOUR TOYS? • UNIT 4   31

Learning goals
- Talk about their favorite toys
- Say which toys make them happy

Main language content
My favorite toy is a train. I like drums.
I don't like the tea set.
Toys: *ball, car, doll, drums, tea set, teddy bear, train*
Numbers: *1-5*

OPENING

Circle time

Materials and preparation
- Puppet
- Visual schedule pictures

Have all the students sit in a circle, facing you. Review the procedures for gathering in a circle. Say *hello* to them and invite them to greet you back.
Place the visual schedule pictures face down in the circle. Say the schedule for the day, one activity at a time, and have different students turn over the cards looking for the picture that represents the activity.

Play *Hear it and bring an object.*

Tell students you will be calling out a number and an object and that they will have to bring it to you. For example, *Five pencils!* – students run to take five pencils and bring them to you. *One red crayon!*, etc. Students can work individually, in pairs, or in groups.

ACTIVE LEARNING

Circle the toys you like to play with.

Materials and preparation
- Project Book page 31

Help students open their Project Book to page 31 and elicit the names of the toys. Give them pencils and ask them to circle the toys that they like to play with. Ask students to tell everyone what toys they have circled.

Count the toys you like to play with. Circle the numbers.

Materials and preparation
- Crayons
- Project Book page 31

Now ask students to count the number of toys they have circled. Ask *How many toys?* Students can answer by telling you the number. Invite students to circle the right number from one to five under the toys. Help them understand the numbers by saying the colors these numbers have. Ask students, *What's your favorite toy?* Help them answer the question by providing the right vocabulary if necessary. *Do toys make you happy? Why? (Because we play and have fun, we get to share them with friends, we use our imagination, etc.)*. Pick students randomly and ask, *Do you like (trains)?* Students answer with *yes* or *no*. Invite students to tell you a toy that they like, *I like dolls*, or don't like, *I don't like trains*.

Note to teachers
Using different colors when writing numbers is a great way to have them introduced to reading numbers. You can also have them use their "writing finger" to trace over the number as you say what color it is.

DIFFERENTIATED INSTRUCTION

BELOW LEVEL

Materials and preparation
- Project Book page 31

Ask students to count the toys and use their fingers to show you the number. Elicit the colors of the toys.

ABOVE LEVEL

Call out a number and have students say what color that number is.

CLOSING

Draw your favorite toy. Say goodbye.

Materials and preparation
- Crayons
- Sheets of paper

Ask students to draw their favorite toy. Give them a sheet of paper and crayons and allow time to draw. Monitor the activity and walk around asking them what they are drawing. When they have finished, invite them to come to the front of the class and tell everyone their favorite toy.
Then wave goodbye to students and ask them what it is time for. Elicit *goodbye* or *bye*.

OPENING

Circle time

Materials and preparation
- Puppet
- Visual schedule pictures

Greet students and have them greet you back. You can use the class puppet and encourage the students to greet the puppet in English. Gather students in a circle and review the procedures for starting each class.
Review the attention-getter: *One, two, three, eyes on me; one, two eyes on you.* Say, *One, two, three, eyes on me* and students should say, *One, two, eyes on you* and look at you at once.
Finally show them the pictures of the visual schedule that correspond to the activities you are doing today.

> **Note to teachers**
> Practice new attention-getters a couple of times.

Draw a train.

Materials and preparation
- Sheets of paper
- Two green, red, and yellow crayons to be put on your desk

Give every student a sheet of paper. Put two red, green, and yellow crayons on your desk for students to share. Tell them to draw a train and color it red, green, and yellow. Teach students to say, *Can I have the red/green/yellow crayon, please?*
Make sure students share the crayons as they are coloring. Teach them to say, *Thank you!* when they get a crayon. When they have finished, encourage them to talk about how they felt having to share the crayons with their classmates.

> **Note to teachers**
> Make sure to model the language that students should use.

Learning goals
- Review vocabulary related to toys and colors
- Learn to share toys

Main language content

Can I have (the doll)?
Let's play together. They are fighting.
Let's share.
How do you feel?
Colors: *blue, green, red, yellow*

Personal, Social, and Emotional Development

ACTIVE LEARNING

What are the children doing?

Materials and preparation

- Crayons
- Project Book page 33

Help students open their Project Book to page 33. Hold up your book, point to the picture. Ask, *What are the children doing?* Help them answer.
Then ask students about their favorite toys. You might ask, for example, *Do you let other children play with your favorite toys?* Draw students' attention to the toys on page 33. Ask, *Are these toys good for playing together?* Talk about working in the yard together and cooking together. Have students understand the importance of sharing and taking good care of everyone's toys.

> **Note to teachers**
> You can also make a list of their favorite toys and display it on the classroom wall.

Draw another play-together toy.

- Crayons
- Project Book page 33

Ask students to tell you about other good play-together toys (e.g., building blocks). Encourage them to share their experiences in sharing their toys with the class.
Then ask students to draw another play-together toy that they often share with other children.
Walk around the classroom to monitor their work. When students have finished, have them show their drawings to their classmates and talk about the toy. Encourage them to explain why that toy is a good play-together toy.

Think! question

Materials and preparation

- Project Book page 33

Ask the *Think!* question: *How do you feel when someone shares with you?* and encourage students to express their opinions.

DIFFERENTIATED INSTRUCTION

BELOW LEVEL
Continue the drawing.

Materials and preparation

- Unfinished drawings depicting toys: prepare them in advance

Organize students into pairs. Ask students to continue the drawings that you started. Give an unfinished drawing to each pair. When students have finished, ask them to color the drawings and talk about them with their classmates.

ABOVE LEVEL
Modern painting

Materials and preparation

- Construction paper
- Paints in different colors
- Sponges

Organize students into groups of three or four. Every group gets one large sheet of construction paper, three or four sponges, and paints in different colors. They should work together to make a modern painting using different colors. When they have finished, encourage them to talk about their modern painting with the class. They should mention the colors they used. Finally display the paintings on the wall when students finish.

CLOSING

Admire art and say goodbye.

Materials and preparation

- Drawings and modern paintings
- Puppet

Take the puppet around the classroom to admire the drawings and the modern paintings and ask about the colors in them. Finally have the puppet praise the students and tell them it is clean-up time. When they have finished cleaning up the classroom, tell students to say *goodbye* to you and to the puppet.

CIRCLE THE PICTURE WHERE THE GIRL IS KIND.

THINK! HOW KIND ARE YOU TO OTHERS?

PERSONAL, SOCIAL, AND EMOTIONAL DEVELOPMENT • DO YOU SHARE YOUR TOYS? • UNIT 4

Learning goals
- Learn to interact with others and respect other's turn
- Use language to talk about being kind or unkind to others

Main language content
It's your turn. She is kind. He is good.
Adjectives: *bad, good, kind, unkind*

OPENING

Circle time
Materials and preparation
- Puppet
- Visual schedule pictures

Greet students and have them greet you and the puppet back. Gather students in a circle and review the procedures for moving safely around the classroom.
Review the attention-getter: *Flat tire, shhhh*. Say, *Flat tire* and have students respond, *shhh* and then they should be quiet and looking at you.
Show students the visual schedule. Have them help you select the pictures that represent the activities they are going to do today and order them.

> **Note to teachers**
> You may play or sing the *Hello song* with students right after they gather in the circle.

Play Splash!
Materials and preparation
- Masking tape

Stick a long piece of masking tape across the floor. Have students walk along it without falling off the line into "the water." After walking across it successfully, they have to hop along it or go tiptoeing along it. If they fall off the line, everyone shouts *Splash!* and they go to the end of the line and wait to have another go.

Personal, Social, and Emotional Development

ACTIVE LEARNING

Circle the picture where the girl is kind.

Materials and preparation
- Crayons
- Project Book page 35

Help students open their Project Book to page 35. Have them talk about the pictures. Ask, *Is the girl kind?* Give them time to look at all the pictures and find out where she is not being kind. Tell the students the story.
T: *Isadora is Noah's sister. Noah is three. Isadora is six.* (Hold up your fingers as you say the number) *Noah is playing with Isadora's...*
S: *ball!*
T: *Isadora says, "That's mine!" Is Noah happy? (Boo, hoo, hoo)!*
S: *No, he isn't.*
T: *Who's this?*
S: *Mommy.*
T: *Yes. And Mommy's not happy! She says, "Isadora! Be nice to Noah!" Is Isadora nice to Noah now?*
S: *Yes!*
T: *What does she say? She says, "It's your turn."*

Help students tell the story in their own words. Then have them circle the picture where Isadora is being kind.

Think! question

Ask the *Think!* question: *How kind are you to others?* Have students first talk to a classmate about it; then invite them to share their answers with the class.

It's your turn!

Materials and preparation
- A large container with sand
- A table spoon
- Five paper plates numbered 1-5
- Resealable sandwich bags (one per student)

Give everybody a resealable sandwich bag. Help them fill it with five spoonfuls of sand. Encourage them to count as they fill their spoons. While helping students, say, *(Student's name), it's your turn now.* Arrange a line with the five plates marked 1-5 on the floor. The first student tries to throw the sand bag onto plate 1, the second onto plate 2, etc. When someone has hit 5, follow down the line from 1 to 5 again. Encourage them to use the expression *It's your turn.*, after trying to throw their bags.

> **Note to teachers**
> If your group is very large, use two containers of sand and two table spoons and arrange students in two lines to fill their bags.

DIFFERENTIATED INSTRUCTION

BELOW LEVEL

Materials and preparation
- Project Book page 35

Make groups of three. Each student will be one of the characters in the story and act it out in front of their classmates.

ABOVE LEVEL

Have students work in groups. Have one of them shout *kind* or *unkind* as the rest find a picture depicting that attitude and repeating the word.

CLOSING

Sing the *Clean-up time* song and say goodbye.

Materials and preparation
- Audio library - songs
- Puppet

Ask students to clean up the classroom. Repeat the *Clean-up time* song (track 11). Have students sing along.
After repeating the song a few times, make sure to say *goodbye* to each one of the students and encourage them to say *goodbye* to the puppet in return.

Unit 5 How do you help at home?

CHECK THE CHORES YOU DO.
CROSS OUT THE CHORES YOU DON'T DO. ✔ ✘

COMPARE WITH A FRIEND.

PERSONAL, SOCIAL, AND EMOTIONAL DEVELOPMENT • HOW DO YOU HELP AT HOME? • UNIT 5   37

Learning goals
- Identify rooms in a house
- Talk about their home and their chores

Main language content
I like to clean. I don't like to mop.
Numbers: *1-6*
House: *bedroom, bathroom, kitchen, living room*
Chores: *make the bed, mop, sweep the floor, wash*

OPENING

Circle time
Materials and preparation
- Puppet
- Visual schedule pictures

Have all the students sit in a circle, facing you. Review the procedures for gathering in a circle. Say *hello* to them and invite them to greet you back. Place the visual schedule pictures face down in the circle. Say the schedule for the day, one activity at a time, and have different students turn over the cards looking for the picture that represents the activity.

My house
Materials and preparation
- Crayons
- Sheets of paper (one per student)

Give each student some paper and colored pencils and ask them to draw their home. Ask, *What shape is your home? Is it a circle? Is it a triangle? Is it a square?*
Ask students how many rooms they have in their home. Can they name the rooms? Have students name one room and try to draw it on the board.

40   Personal, Social, and Emotional Development

ACTIVE LEARNING

Check the chores you do. Cross out the chores you don't do.

Materials and preparation
- Project Book page 37

Help students open their Project Book to page 37 and ask them to look at the pictures. *What are the children doing?* Elicit the names of the chores in the pictures (*sweep the floor, make my bed, set the table, pick up my toys, feed my pet*).
Ask students to think whether they do these chores at home, check the ones that they do and put an X on the ones that they don't.

Compare with a friend.

Have students work in pairs to tell their classmate what they do and don't do at home. *I sweep the floor. I wash clothes. I set the table.*, etc. Students then ask each other, *What do you like to do? I like to pick up my toys!*
Discuss with the class the importance of doing chores at home, *Why do you do chores?* Explain that doing chores from a young age is a good way to learn how to be responsible and have discipline, both very important qualities.

DIFFERENTIATED INSTRUCTION

BELOW LEVEL

Have everyone stand up and make a circle. Call out names of chores and have students pretend they are doing these chores.

ABOVE LEVEL

Have students present themselves to the whole class and talk about the chores they do at home. *I make my bed. I sweep the floor.*

CLOSING

My bedroom

Materials and preparation
- Crayons
- Sheets of paper (one per student)

Give paper and pencils and ask students to draw their bedroom. Hang the drawings around the classroom and go around with students eliciting the shapes they can see in the drawings.

Goodbye time

Say *goodbye* to students and have them say *goodbye* back to you.

WHO HELPS AT HOME? CHECK.

PERSONAL, SOCIAL, AND EMOTIONAL DEVELOPMENT • HOW DO YOU HELP AT HOME? • UNIT 5   39

Learning goals
- Talk about chores they can and can't do
- Learn about the importance of helping others at home with chores

Main language content
House: *bathroom, bed, bedroom, chair, kitchen, living room, table*
Chores: *clean, mop, sweep, wash*
Family: *brother, daddy, mommy, sister*

OPENING

Circle time

Materials and preparation
- Puppet
- Visual schedule pictures

Have all the students sit in a circle, facing you. Review the procedures for gathering in a circle. Say *hello* to them and invite them to greet you back. Show students the visual schedule pictures. Tell them the schedule for the day and have them point to the picture that represents each of the activities.

Let's mime!

Tell students that you are going to mime a household chore and they need to name it. Pretend that you are sweeping the floor and elicit the expression from students. Invite other students to come forward and mime, too.

Personal, Social, and Emotional Development

ACTIVE LEARNING

Who helps at home? Check.

Materials and preparation
- Crayons or pencils
- Project Book page 39

Help students open their Project Book to page 39 and ask them to take a look at the pictures with you. *What chores do you see? Who is washing the dishes? Who is mopping the floor?* Students answer the questions by naming the chores and the members of the family.
Ask students if they help at home when another family member does chores: *Who do you help? What do you do?*
Ask students to check the pictures where family members are helping each other do the house chores. Ask them, *Are they happy or sad?*

Learn to help each other.

Materials and preparation
- Brooms
- Cleaning cloths

Divide students into small groups and place each group in a specific spot in the classroom. Make sure there is something to clean or organize in each spot. Explain that each group is a family and they need to help each other clean their little spot. Give out brooms and cleaning cloths and invite them to decide who is doing what in order to clean their spot.

> **Note to teachers**
> This activity is a great way to teach students about team work and the importance of helping their family and their classmates to clean the house or classroom.

DIFFERENTIATED INSTRUCTION

BELOW LEVEL

Materials and preparation
- Project Book page 39

Call out a chore and ask students to point to it on Project Book page 39.

ABOVE LEVEL

Ask students about the rooms where the family members are in each picture and what chores are done in each room.

CLOSING

Make a chore poster. Say goodbye.

Materials and preparation
- Butcher or poster paper
- Crayons
- Puppet

Invite students to tell (in pairs or groups) what they can and cannot do at home. For example, *I can sweep the floor/I can´t do the dishes*. Then give them a piece of butcher paper and ask them to make a chore poster by drawing some of the chores they do at home.
Then say *goodbye* to students and encourage them to say *goodbye* to you and the puppet.

OPENING

Circle time
Materials and preparation
- Calendar
- Puppet
- Visual schedule pictures

Say *hello* to students and have them say *hello* back to you. Invite them to sit in a circle and say *Hi* or *Hello* to the student next to them. Make sure everybody has been greeted.
Say the attention-getter: *Listen, carefully*. When you say, *Listen*, students respond, *Carefully*.
Show students the calendar. Go through the calendar routine, looking at the day today and the date.
Bring the visual schedule pictures and place them facing down in the circle. Ask students to find the right picture as you read the schedule for the day.

Introducing the theme
Materials and preparation
- Colored pencils
- Sheets of paper

Give each student a sheet of paper. Have them draw their bedroom and some of the furniture they have. Tell them to circle their bed. Walk around and praise their work.

Learning goals
- Understand and reproduce the steps of making the bed
- Talk about the toys they sleep with

Main language content
Shake the sheet. Make the bed.
Put the sheet on the bed.
Put the comforter on the bed.
Put the pillow on the bed.
Put your pajamas under the pillow.
Put your cuddly toy on the bed.
What's your favorite cuddly toy?
Toys: doll, teddy bear

Personal, Social, and Emotional Development

ACTIVE LEARNING

Learn to make your bed.

Materials and preparation

- A toy bed, sheet, pillow, doll's pajamas, comforter
- Flashcard: *bed*
- Pencils

Hold up the flashcard of the bed and say, *This is a bed*. Have students repeat.
Say, *This is how we make the bed*. Get out the toy bed, the sheet, the comforter, the pillow, and doll's pajamas. Say, *Shake the sheet. Put the sheet on the bed. Then put the comforter on the bed. After that put the pillow on the bed. Finally put your pajamas under the pillow*.
Repeat the procedure and have students repeat each sentence after you. Do it a few times to make sure students learn the new vocabulary.

Do you make your own bed? Listen and order the pictures.

Materials and preparation

- Audio library - class content
- Pencils
- Project Book page 41

Help students open their Project Book to page 41. Ask, *Do you make your own bed?* Allow everyone to answer. Remind students to respect their classmates answer, as answers may be different. Read the rubrics and explain to students what they have to do. Play the audio (track 04) twice, if necessary.

Audio script

1. *Shake the sheet.*
2. *Put the sheet on the bed.*
3. *Put the comforter on the bed.*
4. *Put the pillow on the bed.*
5. *Put your pajamas under the pillow.*
6. *Put your cuddly toy on the bed.*

Note to teachers

Practice the sentences a couple of times before expecting students to repeat them. Repetition helps students make connections between phrases and meaning besides helping them practice their pronunciation.

What toys do you sleep with?

Ask students, *What toys do you sleep with?* Help them with the answers. Make sure everybody participates.

DIFFERENTIATED INSTRUCTION

BELOW LEVEL
Miming activity

In pairs, ask students to mime to each other the steps of making a bed. One at a time, then they take turns.

ABOVE LEVEL
Making a bed

Have students work in groups of six. Each member of the group should act and describe one step in making a bed and the others have to try to guess.

CLOSING

Talk about your cuddly toy. Sing the *Goodbye song*.

Materials and preparation

- Audio library - songs
- Puppet

Put on the puppet. Walk around the room and have him ask students about their favorite cuddly toys: *What cuddly toys go to bed with you?*
Invite students to sing the *Goodbye song* (track 05). Say *goodbye* to students and have them say *goodbye* to you and the puppet.

TALK ABOUT THE PICTURES. ACT OUT THE SITUATIONS.

DRAW WHAT YOU DO TO HELP AT HOME.

THINK! WHAT CHORES ARE FUN TO DO?

PERSONAL, SOCIAL, AND EMOTIONAL DEVELOPMENT • HOW DO YOU HELP AT HOME? • UNIT 5 43

Learning goals
- Talk about chores
- Accept and follow rules

Main language content

*Help me make your bed.
Come and help me.
Yes, mommy. Yes, daddy.*

OPENING

Circle time

Materials and preparation
- Puppet
- Visual schedule pictures

Greet students and have them greet you and the puppet back. Gather students in a circle and review the procedures for moving safely around the classroom.
Show students the visual schedule. Have them help you select the pictures that represent the activities they are going to do today and order them.

Chore words

Materials and preparation
- Soft ball

Tell students to sit around you. Roll a soft ball to one of them. The student picks up the ball, says a word or phrase connected with chores, and rolls the ball back to you. Roll the ball to another student and continue. It does not matter if the chores get repeated. Then talk to students about their obligations at home: making their beds, putting away their toys, etc.

> **Note to teachers**
> Praise students for the things they do to help at home. Also, remind them of how important it is to keep our homes, school, etc. clean and neat.

Personal, Social, and Emotional Development

ACTIVE LEARNING

Talk about the pictures. Act out the situations.

Materials and preparation.
- Crayons
- Project Book page 43

Help students open their Project Book to page 43. Have them look at the pictures and say what is happening. Then teach students the following conversation:

Dad: *Come and help me.*
Boy: *Yes, Daddy.*
Dad: *Help me make your bed.*
Boy: *Yes, Daddy.*

After that, divide the class into two groups: one group is the dad and the other group is the little boy. Help students practice the conversation chorally like this until they have learned it. Then have students act out the conversation in pairs. Go around helping them. Ask, *Is the boy happy to help his dad?* Say, *Yes. It's good to help.*
After students have acted out the conversation in pairs, have them look at the other pictures. Ask them what they think is being said. Let them come up with the sentences themselves.

Probable conversations:
Mom: *Come and help me.*
Girl: *Yes, Mommy.*
Mom: *Help me wash the car.*
Girl: *Yes, Mommy.*

Dad: *Come and help me.*
Girl: *Yes, Daddy.*
Dad: *Help me sweep the kitchen floor.*
Girl: *Yes, Daddy.*

Draw what you do to help at home.

Materials and preparation
- Crayons or pencils
- Project Book page 43

Draw students' attention to the frame on the page. Ask them what chores they do to help at home. Then tell them they will draw a picture of someone in their family asking for help with a chore. Go around asking about their pictures.

Think! question

Ask the *Think!* question: *What chores are fun to do?* Have students first talk to a classmate about it; then invite them to share their answers with the class and see if they agree.

DIFFERENTIATED INSTRUCTION

BELOW LEVEL

Materials and preparation
- Crayons or pencils
- Project Book page 43
- Sheets of paper (one per student)

If students have a hard time coming up with chores, have them think of chores in pairs and draw one they find there. Say the name of a chore and have them point to it if they have it.

ABOVE LEVEL

Materials and preparation
- Crayons or pencils
- Project Book page 43
- Sheets of paper (one per student)

Tell students they will work in pairs and tell each other what they have drawn. Their classmate will pretend to be doing that chore. Have them also come up with other chores for their classmates to act out.

CLOSING

Tell the puppet what you do. Say goodbye.

Materials and preparation
- Puppet

Tell students the puppet wants to know what they do to help at home. Have the puppet first ask the question and, as students answer, have it say, *Good boy/girl!* Then you and the puppet say *goodbye!* to students.

Unit 6 How do you take care of your pet?

LISTEN AND NUMBER THE PICTURES.

PERSONAL, SOCIAL, AND EMOTIONAL DEVELOPMENT • HOW DO YOU TAKE CARE OF YOUR PET? • UNIT 6

Learning goals
- Understand the sequence of a story
- Learn how to take care of pets
- Understand and follow commands

Main language content
Come here! Sit down! Leave it! Stay!
Dog, pet, puppy,
Train
Colors: *blue, red, orange, pink*

OPENING

Circle time

Materials and preparation
- Puppet
- Visual schedule pictures

Have all the students sit in a circle, facing you. Review the procedures for gathering in a circle. Say *hello* to them and invite them to greet you back.
Place the visual schedule pictures face down in the circle. Say the schedule for the day, one activity at a time, and have different students turn over the cards looking for the picture that represents the activity.

> **Note to teachers**
> This lesson talks about pets and students' relationship with pets. Although a few activities suggest that they talk about their pets, you can always have them think of their experience with pets around them, in their neighborhood, at a friend's house, or at a relative's house.

Wash, wash, wash

Materials and preparation
- Brushes
- Dirt or soil from the yard (or clay)
- Plastic animal toys
- Soap
- Towels
- Two plastic containers

Talk to students about how we should take care of our pets. One basic rule is to keep them clean. Present both containers to the students. Put dirt and water and all the animal toys in one and soap and water in the other. Tell students they should wash the animals and take care of them just like they would with their own pets.

48 Personal, Social, and Emotional Development

ACTIVE LEARNING

Listen and number the pictures.

Materials and preparation
- Project Book page 45

Help students open their Project Book to page 45. Talk to students about what they can see in the pictures (the boy is giving commands to his dog). Make sure they understand the meaning of *Stay*, *Sit down*, *Leave it*, and *Come here*. Tell students you are going to play an audio with the commands and they have to number the pictures in the right order. Allow time for students to order the pictures.
When everyone is ready, play the audio (track 05) twice. Make sure students find the right picture.

Audio script 🎧 05

Boy: *Stay!*
Boy: *Leave it!*
Boy: *Come here!*
Boy: *Sit down.*

> **Note to teachers**
> If students struggle to write the numbers, have them draw tally marks instead: one tally for number one, two tallies for number two, etc.

Draw a puppy.

Materials and preparation
- Colored pens

Ask students to turn their paper over and draw a puppy. They can take this drawing home and show their parents the commands the puppy knows.

DIFFERENTIATED INSTRUCTION

BELOW LEVEL

Materials and preparation
- Project Book page 45

Ask students to identify the pet and colors in the pictures.

ABOVE LEVEL

Ask the students to identify the command in each picture.

CLOSING

Play *Teacher says*.

This game is a variation of *Simon says* where you use the four commands from the *Active learning* activity and students pretend to be the pet and follow the command, but only if the command starts with *The teacher says...*

Sing the *Goodbye song*.

Materials and preparation
- Audio library - songs

Sing the *Goodbye song* (track 05) as you are waving goodbye to students.

> **Note to teachers**
> For next class: send a note to parents asking for a picture of students' homes.

MATCH EACH ANIMAL WITH THEIR HABITAT.

PERSONAL, SOCIAL, AND EMOTIONAL DEVELOPMENT • HOW DO YOU TAKE CARE OF YOUR PET? • UNIT 6 47

Learning goals
- Associate animals with their habitats
- Understand that they need to take care of their pets

Main language content
I have a cat. He has a hamster.
Pets: *bird, cat, dog, fish, hamster, parrot, rabbit, turtle*
Pet needs: *fly, sleep, swim, walk, water*

OPENING

Circle time

Materials and preparation
- Puppet
- Visual schedule pictures

Have all the students sit in a circle, facing you. Review the procedures for gathering in a circle. Say *hello* to them and invite them to greet you back.

Hide the visual schedule pictures and have students look for them. When they find the pictures, tell them to bring them back to the circle. Tell them the schedule for the day and have them point to the picture that represents each of the activities.

Find the pet!

Materials and preparation
- Flashcards: *cat, dog, fish, turtle*
- Masking tape

Fix the flashcards/pictures of pets with sticky tape around the classroom. Tell students you have put up pictures of pets and that they should go around, find them, point at them, and call out the pet name.

When all pets have been identified, collect the pictures and hold them up one by one. Call out students' names and elicit the pet name one more time.

Ask students, *Do you have a pet?* Students answer, *Yes, I have a (dog).* or *No.*

ACTIVE LEARNING

Match each animal with their habitat.

Materials and preparation

- Picture of students' homes
- Project Book page 47

Invite students to present the picture of their home. Explain to them that animals also have homes, we call them *habitats* and they are very similar to the ones we humans live in.

Help students open their Project Book to page 47. Elicit from students the names of the animals. Ask, *What is this? It is a fish!* Then draw students' attention to the animal habitats on the right side of the picture. Ask if they can guess or identify which animal lives in each habitat.

Ask students to draw a line and connect each animal to their habitat.

Water animals

Materials and preparation

- A plastic fish or laminated paper fish
- Small plastic tubs or one big plastic tub

Put the plastic tub full of water in the middle of the classroom. Ask students, *What animal lives in the water?* Encourage them to answer, *Fish*. Give out the plastic fish and let them put them in the water and play.

DIFFERENTIATED INSTRUCTION

BELOW LEVEL

Materials and preparation

- Project Book page 47

Ask students to work in groups to come up with the names of two more pets and their habitats.

ABOVE LEVEL

Ask students to identify elements of the habitats on page 47 of their Project Book. For example, *water, grass, tree*, etc.

CLOSING

Play *Musical pets*.

Materials and preparation

- Audio library - songs

Play a song of students' choice and encourage them to dance around the classroom. When you stop the music, hold up the picture of a pet and tell them to use body language to do something related to this pet. For example, the sounds it makes, the way it walks, the way it sleeps, etc.

Goodbye time

Say *goodbye* to each student by giving them a hug and waving goodbye.

IS EVERYONE KIND TO ANIMALS?
WHAT DO PETS NEED?

WHAT ANIMALS NEED HELP? CIRCLE.

PERSONAL, SOCIAL, AND EMOTIONAL DEVELOPMENT • HOW DO YOU TAKE CARE OF YOUR PET? • UNIT 6 — 49

Learning goals
- Recognize when someone needs help
- Name pets and ask questions about them

Main language content
What's your (dog's) name?
Do you have a bird?
How old is (he)?
Where does (he) live?
What color is (he)?
Animals: *bird, cat, dog, fish, lion, pig, shark, turtle*
Feelings: *angry, happy, sad*

OPENING

Circle time
Materials and preparation
- Feelings chart
- Puppet
- Visual schedule pictures

Gather students in a circle and go over the procedures for the beginning of the class. Review how to sit properly, walk safely, and move around the classroom.
Ask students to greet the classmate sitting next to them and ask, *How are you today?* Refer to the Feelings chart to help them answer. Bring the visual schedule pictures and place them face down in the circle. Ask students to find the right picture as you read the schedule for the day.

Sing *Why is that doggie in the window?*
Materials and preparation
- Audio library - songs

Gather students in a circle and teach them the song *Why is that doggie in the window?* (track 22). Play it a couple of times and have them sing along. Gesture while singing the lyrics so that they can learn.

Personal, Social, and Emotional Development

ACTIVE LEARNING

Is everyone kind to animals? What do pets need?

Materials and preparation
- Project Book page 49

Help students open their Project Book to page 49. Hold your book and point to the picture at the top of the page. Elicit a description of the picture from students, including feelings and reasons for them. Ask students what pets need. As they give suggestions, make simple drawings on the board, for example, of a house, a basket, a heart, and food. Students can then use the pictures as cues to talk about what pets need to be happy.

Hold the book again and show the picture of the sad animals once more. Ask students why they think these animals are sad. Allow students to give their opinion freely.

> **Note to teachers**
> Some questions can raise a heated discussion among students. When that happens, it is essential to teach them to listen and respect their classmate's opinion. Remind students that everyone is different and thinks in a different way.

What animals need help? Circle.

Materials and preparation
- Crayons
- Project Book page 49

Draw student's attention to the two pictures at the bottom half of the page. Ask them to describe the pictures and then have them circle the picture of the dogs that need help. Elicit reasons for their choice. Focus on the trash all over the street and the fact that these animals seem not to have a home or food.

DIFFERENTIATED INSTRUCTION

BELOW LEVEL
Draw your pet.

Materials and preparation
- Crayons
- Sheets of paper (one per student)

In pairs, have students draw their pets on the sheet or a pet they would like to have. Have them color the drawing, too. Then have them ask each other questions about the animal, *What animal is it? What color is it?* Make sure to model first and monitor the activity.

ABOVE LEVEL

Have students do the same activity as the one described in *Below level*, but make sure to elicit more questions from them: *What animal is it? What color is it? Is it big or small? What's your (bird's) name?* Make sure to model first and monitor the activity.

> **Note to teachers**
> If students don't have a pet, they can draw a pet they would like to have. Allow students to use their imagination whenever a situation doesn't fit into their own reality.

CLOSING

Sing *Why is that doggie in the window?* and say goodbye.

Materials and preparation
- Audio library - songs
- Puppet

Tell students that in some stories dogs run after the mail carrier. Say, *Dogs don't like mail carriers very much*. Ask them why they think that is. Allow students to be creative in their answers. Then say, *Dogs protect their owners and their house. Dogs see mail carriers as invaders, so sometimes they bark at them*. Have students pretend they are dogs barking angrily at a mail carrier. Then have students sing *Why is that doggie in the window?* again (track 22).
When the song ends, ask students to say *Goodbye! See you later!* to their classmates, the puppet, and you.

Unit 6

Learning goals

- Recognize when someone needs help
- Distinguish between a doctor and a vet

Main language content

What does a vet do?
What does a vet give?
Who does the vet wash?
What does the vet cut?
What else does the vet cut?

OPENING

Circle time

Materials and preparation

- Audio library - songs
- Puppet
- Visual schedule pictures

Greet students and have them greet you and the puppet back. Gather students in a circle and review the procedures for moving safely around the classroom. Play the *Hello song* (track 04) and have students sing along.
Bring the visual schedule pictures and place them facing down in the circle. Ask students to find the right picture as you read the schedule for the day.

My dog is sick!

Materials and preparation

- A toy dog

Show students a toy dog. Hold it up in front of your face and sneeze. Say, *Oh, dear! My dog is sick! What can we do?* Wait for students to suggest things, accepting ideas in L1. Elicit *go to the vet*. Ask them to repeat the word *vet*.

Personal, Social, and Emotional Development

ACTIVE LEARNING

Look at the pictures. What is a vet? What does a vet do?

Materials and preparation
- Crayons
- Project Book page 51

Help students open their Project Book to page 51. Have them look at the picture and talk about the animals they can see. Then hold your book up in front of the class and ask, *Who is a vet? What does a vet do?* Say, *Let's find out what a vet does.* Then read the facts below about vets. *A vet looks after sick animals. The vet gives vaccinations. The vet washes dogs. The vet cuts animals' fur. The vet cuts animals' nails.* When you finish telling them the facts, ask students the following questions:
What does a vet do?
What does a vet give?
Who does the vet looks after?

Circle what a doctor does.

Materials and preparation
- Crayons or pencils
- Project Book page 51

Draw students' attention to the two pictures at the bottom of the page. Ask them to describe the picture and then have them circle the picture that shows what a doctor does. Elicit reasons for their choice.

Think! question

Ask the *Think!* question: *When do you see a doctor?* Have students first talk to a classmate about it; then invite them to share their answers with the class.

Note to teachers
Students may find it difficult to talk about specific illnesses or symptoms, so as they point or try to describe, point to a given part of your body and repeat after them in English.

DIFFERENTIATED INSTRUCTION

BELOW LEVEL
Divide students into small groups. Have students take turns to say either *vet* or *doctor*. The others have to say something that this person does.

ABOVE LEVEL
Have a student come to the front and say something that a vet or a doctor does, e.g., *I cut the dog's nails.* Then have the other students say whether the person is a vet or a doctor.

CLOSING

Review what you've learned. Say goodbye.

Materials and preparation
- Audio library - songs
- Puppet
- Soft ball

Have students sit in a circle around you. Roll a ball to one of them. The student who picks up the ball will say a word they learned in the previous lessons and roll it back to you. Roll the ball to another student. Continue until no one can think of any more words. Finally, play the *Goodbye song* (track 05) and have students sing along while waving goodbye to you and the puppet.

Unit 7 What is your favorite food?

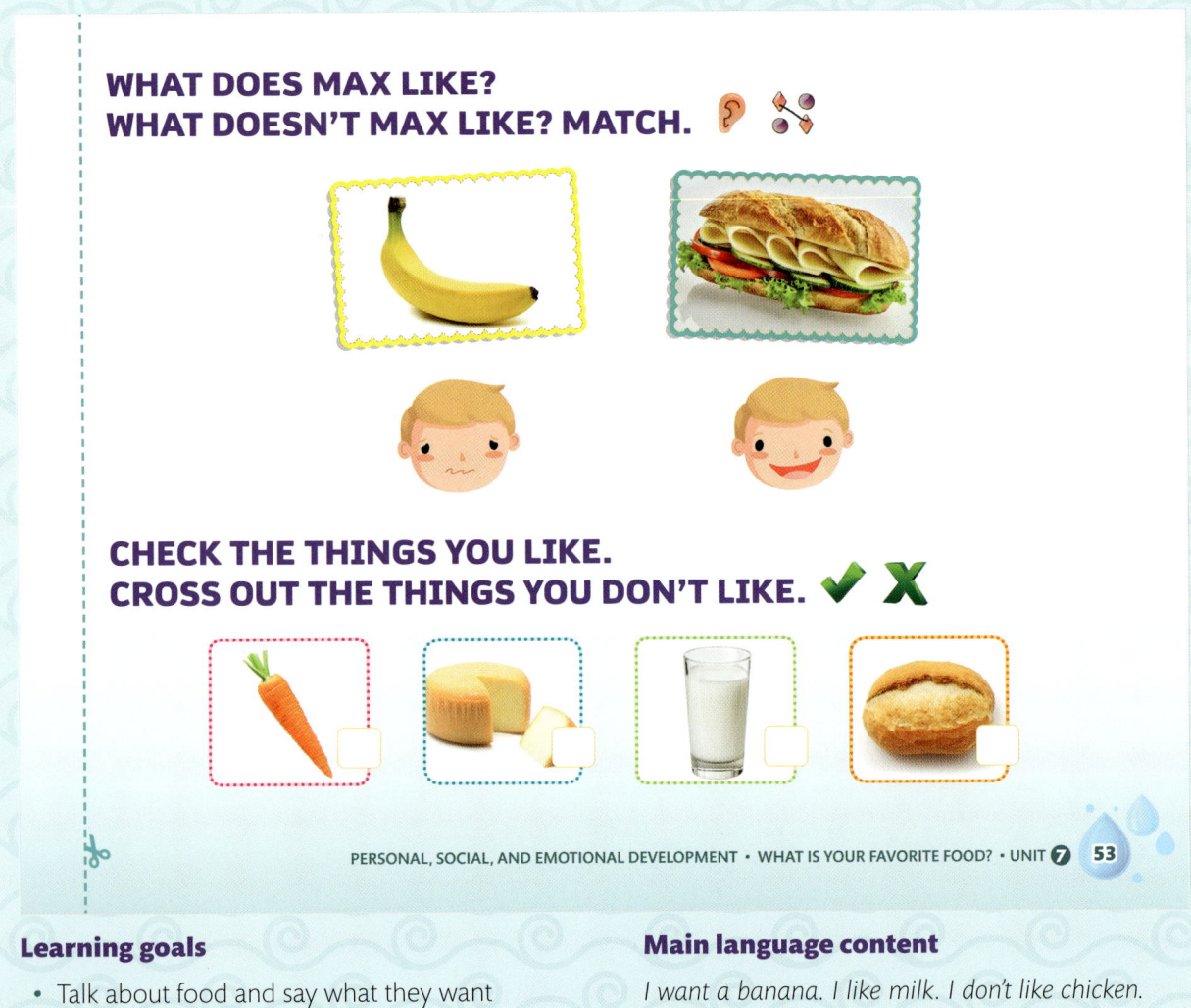

Learning goals
- Talk about food and say what they want
- Talk about likes and dislikes

Main language content
I want a banana. I like milk. I don't like chicken.
Food and drinks: *apple, banana, bread, carrot, cereal, cheese, chicken, grapes, milk, tomato, water*

OPENING

Circle time

Materials and preparation
- Puppet
- Visual schedule pictures

Have all the students sit in a circle, facing the teacher. Review the procedures for gathering in a circle. Say *hello* to them and invite them to greet you back.
Show students the visual schedule pictures. Tell them the schedule for the day and have them point to the picture that represents each of the activities.

> **Note to teachers**
> The next four lessons talk about food and eating habits. Make sure to deal with this topic carefully as students have different diets and may differ in opinion when it comes to what is considered healthy and unhealthy. They may also like and dislike different food items, so help them understand that being different and having different tastes is natural.

Name the food!

Materials and preparation
- Balloons
- Pictures of food items students are familiar with such as *apple, banana, bread, cereal,* etc.
- String

Place a small picture inside each balloon and blow them up. Use string to attach a balloon to each student's leg. Explain to students that the idea of the game is to try to burst a classmates' balloon, pick up the picture and call out the name of the food.

Personal, Social, and Emotional Development

ACTIVE LEARNING

What does Max like? What doesn't Max like? Match.

Materials and preparation
- Crayons or pencils
- Project Book page 53

Help students open their Project Book to page 53. Hold up your book, point to the picture of the boy and say, *This is Max*. Point to the picture of Max under the food items and elicit whether Max is happy or not. Tell students that you are going to speak as Max and they have to match the faces that shows Max's likes or dislikes with the correct food item.
Max: *I like bananas.*
I don't like sandwiches.
Read Max's phrases again and ask students to repeat after you.

Check the things you like. Cross out the things you don't like.

Materials and preparation
- Crayons and pencils
- Project Book page 53

Make a large checkmark and an X on the board. Ask students to take a look at the second group of pictures, check what they like and cross out what they don't like. Divide students into pairs and have them tell each other about their likes and dislikes from the second group of pictures. For example, *I like cheese. I don't like milk.*

DIFFERENTIATED INSTRUCTION

BELOW LEVEL

Materials and preparation
- Project Book page 53

Hold up your book and ask students which face shows Max's likes and which one shows Max's dislikes.

ABOVE LEVEL

Ask students individually what they checked and what they crossed out. They need to tell the whole class what they like and what they don't like.

CLOSING

Mystery boxes

Materials and preparation
- Four square, cardboard boxes big enough for students to put their hands inside (suggestion: coffee capsules come in such boxes)
- Real food for each box such as fruit, vegetables or whatever you can bring to class that students are familiar with paper to wrap the boxes
- Wrapping paper

Wrap each box and make a hole big enough for the students to put their hands inside. Place some type of food inside the box. Bring the boxes forward and explain to students that you have put food inside the boxes and they need to use their hands to find out what food it is. You can divide the class into two groups that can compete against each other or each student can play for themselves. Students put their hands inside and touch the food. They can hold the food in their hand but not take it out of the box to see what it is. Each group/student who identifies the food gets a point.

Sing the *Goodbye song*.

Materials and preparation
- Audio library - songs

Sing the *Goodbye song* (track 05) with students and have them say *goodbye* to you.

COLOR THE HEALTHY FOOD.

PERSONAL, SOCIAL, AND EMOTIONAL DEVELOPMENT • WHAT IS YOUR FAVORITE FOOD? • UNIT 7 · 55

Learning goals
- Talk about food that is good for them
- Take care of themselves and others

Main language content
Can I have a carrot? The banana is yellow.
Food and drinks: *apple, banana, bread, carrot, chicken, chocolate, grapes, milk, sandwich, soda, tomato, water*

OPENING

Circle time

Materials and preparation
- Puppet
- Visual schedule pictures

Have all the students sit in a circle, facing you. Review the procedures for gathering in a circle. Say *hello* to them and invite them to greet you back.
Hide the visual schedule pictures and have students look for them. When they find the pictures, tell them to bring them back to the circle. Tell them the schedule for the day and have them point to the picture that represents each of the activities.

Name the food.

Materials and preparation
- Blindfolds
- Several kinds of food students are known to eat

Cut up different types of fruit and put them in a bowl. Have students sit in a circle and blindfold them or ask them to tightly close their eyes.
Have the bowl passed from one student to the other. Students need to take a piece of fruit, eat it and tell you the name of the fruit.
Make a class survey as to which fruit they liked the best.
Ask, *What color is it? What is the name of the fruit?*

> **Note to teachers**
> Remember to check with parents for any allergies or food intolerance students might have.

Personal, Social, and Emotional Development

ACTIVE LEARNING

Color the healthy food.

Materials and preparation

- Crayons or pencils
- Project Book page 55

Help students open their Project Book to page 55. Point to the doctor in the middle of the page and ask, *Who is this?* Students answer, *It's a doctor!* Tell students to now take a look at the food surrounding the doctor. Point to each food and elicit their names.

Tell students the doctor is going to ask them questions like, *Is water good for you?* And they need to answer with *yes* or *no*. Tell them that you will be the doctor asking the questions, *Is an apple good for you? Is tomato good for you? Is soda good for you? Is chocolate good for you?*

Then, ask students to color the pictures. Walk around and ask, *What colors do you want?*

DIFFERENTIATED INSTRUCTION

BELOW LEVEL

Materials and preparation

- Project Book page 55

Have students ask each other about the food in the pictures: *What is it? It's chocolate!*

ABOVE LEVEL

Divide students into pairs. Explain that in this activity one is the doctor and the other is a patient. The patient asks the doctor, *Can I have an ice cream?* And the doctor replies accordingly, in this case with *No*.

CLOSING

Sing *Pat a cake*.

Materials and preparation

- Audio library - songs

Play the song (track 24) and invite students to sing along and dance! Teach them the movements to mix, stir, pat, and roll.

Say goodbye.

Materials and preparation

- Puppet

Have students come to you one by one to tell you goodbye before they leave the classroom. Ask students, *Does the puppet get a goodbye, too?* Encourage them to say *goodbye* to the puppet.

LOOK AT THE PICTURE AND LISTEN.

WHAT DOES DIANA NEED TO DO? STICK.

THINK! HOW DO YOU STAY CLEAN?

PERSONAL, SOCIAL, AND EMOTIONAL DEVELOPMENT • WHAT IS YOUR FAVORITE FOOD? • UNIT 7   57

Learning goals
- Understand a story and talk about personal hygiene
- Learn and practice vocabulary related to personal hygiene

Main language content
Wash your hands.
Take a shower.
Brush your teeth.
Hygiene: *bath, clean, dirty, shower*

OPENING

Circle time

Materials and preparation
- Puppet
- Visual schedule pictures

Greet students and encourage them to greet you back. Gather them in a circle and review the procedures for moving safely around the classroom.
Hide the visual schedule pictures and have students look for them. When they have found all the pictures, place them in the circle. Call on a student to be the class helper of the day and get the right pictures as you read the schedule.

Getting dirty

Materials and preparation
- Soil or clay

Bring out some soil or clay to the classroom. Have students pass it around and put one of their hands on it to get them dirty. Remind them not to touch anything with their dirty hands.
Then have everyone show both of their hands. Ask, *Which hand is dirty?* and encourage them to show only their dirty hand. Ask about the clean hand, too.
Finally, play *Clean or dirty* with students. When you say *clean*, they will raise their clean hand; when you say *dirty*, they will raise their dirty hand.

Wash your hands.

Materials and preparation
- School washing facilities or buckets with water and pieces of cloth

After the game, ask students, *And now? How can we clean the other hand to get our books?* Allow them to give suggestions and show consideration for all of their ideas.
Take students to the washing facilities or use buckets filled with water to have them wash their hands.

60 Personal, Social, and Emotional Development

ACTIVE LEARNING

Look at the picture and listen.

Materials and preparation
- Audio library - class content
- Project Book page 57

Help students open their Project Book to page 57. Hold up your book in front of the class and point to the picture of the little girl. Say, *This is Diana. Can you repeat her name?* Tell students that Diana is going to her grandma's house today. Then have them repeat the place by asking, *Where's she going?*
Invite them to look at the picture carefully. Ask, *What's the matter with Diana?* Tell the story using different voices for each character. Then play the audio (track 06) and have they listen again.

Audio script

Mom: *We're going to Grandma's house.*
Diana: *My hands are dirty.*
Mom: *Let's wash your hands.*
Diana: *My hair's a mess!*
Mom: *Let's brush your hair.*
Diana: *There's chocolate on my shorts.*
Mom: *Let's change your shorts.*
Diana: *OK, Mommy! Let's go!*

What does Diana need to do? Stick.

Materials and preparation
- Crayons or pencils
- Project Book page 57
- Unit 7 stickers

Draw students' attention to the pictures in the stickers. Tell them that some of these things show what Diana needs to do. Ask, *Does Diana need to wash her hands?* Give special emphasis to the phrase *wash her hands*. As students answer, have them stick this picture in the corresponding place on page 57. Repeat with *eat spaghetti* and *change her shorts*. Monitor and help as needed.

DIFFERENTIATED INSTRUCTION

BELOW LEVEL

Materials and preparation
- Project Book page 57

Ask students the *Think!* question: *How do you stay clean?* Have everyone give their opinion to the whole group and ask follow-up questions about how many times a day they wash their hands, if they have a shower every day, etc.

ABOVE LEVEL

Ask the *Think!* question: *How do you stay clean?* Have them answer the question in groups of three. Walk around and help them with the language needed. Then invite groups to get together with another group and see if they have similar hygiene habits.

CLOSING

Sing the *Goodbye song* and mime.

Materials and preparation
- Audio library - songs

Gather students back in the circle. Explain that they will sing the *Goodbye song* (track 05) and clap with you. As you pause the song, they will stop singing and clapping and pretend to be doing something you tell them to: *Wash your hands. Wash your face. Brush your teeth. Take a shower.*
Play the song again, this time nonstop, and wave goodbye to students.

> **Note to teachers**
>
> Varying the movements and gestures used in a song is a fun way of working with drilling. You can usually take any song students like and work with different gestures and language.

LISTEN. CIRCLE THE FOOD SOME CHILDREN DON'T LIKE.

DRAW FOOD YOU LIKE FOR YOUR PARTY.

THINK! DO YOU SHARE FOOD WITH YOUR FRIENDS? WHY?

PERSONAL, SOCIAL, AND EMOTIONAL DEVELOPMENT • WHAT IS YOUR FAVORITE FOOD? • UNIT 7

Learning goals
- Talk about food they like and dislike
- Talk about party food
- Understand that people have different tastes

Main language content
What food do you like for your party?
I like pizza.
I don't like cupcakes.
Party food: *cake, cupcakes, hotdog, ice cream, pizza, sandwiches*

OPENING

Circle time

Materials and preparation
- Puppet
- Visual schedule pictures

Say *hello* to students and have them greet you back. Encourage them to greet the puppet, too. Ask how they are and help them answer with the words they know.
Bring the visual schedule pictures and place them in the circle. Ask a volunteer to help you get the pictures as you read the schedule for the day.

Party food

Materials and preparation
- Puppet

Review the attention-getter *Hands on top, everybody stop*. Say, *Hands on top* and have students raise their hands and respond, *everybody stop*. Then have the puppet ask students, *What is good food for a party?* Elicit words such as *cake, ice cream, hot dogs, sandwiches*. Have the puppet say, *Good food for a party is food that everybody likes*.

> **Note to teachers**
> It is important to make it clear that good food for a party should not be the only food we eat in everyday life, and that dietary balance is fundamental.

Personal, Social, and Emotional Development

ACTIVE LEARNING

Listen. Circle the food some children don't like.

Materials and preparation
- Audio library - class content
- Crayons
- Project Book page 59

Help students turn to page 59 from their Project Book and ask them what is happening in the picture. Elicit as many words as possible from them.
Ask, *What party food can you see?* Have students talk about the pictures. Tell students they are going to hear about Lucy's party. Tell the story, stopping to ask questions to help students understand. Then tell students that they have to circle the food some children do not like. Play the audio (track 07), and pause whenever students have to circle.

Audio script

Lucy's Party

Lucy: *What are we eating at my party?*
Mom: *Pizza.*
Lucy: *Ronnie and Timmy don't like pizza.*
Mom: *Oh! Let's make sandwiches, too.*
Lucy: *What else are we eating at my party?*
Mom: *Cupcakes.*
Lucy: *Felicity doesn't like cupcakes.*
Mom: *Oh! Let's have ice cream, too.*
Lucy: *What's Dissy eating at my party?*
Narrator: *Dissy is her dog.*
Mom: *Dissy's eating a special treat.*
Narrator: *Everyone is happy. Everyone likes the food.*

Think! question

Materials and preparation
- Project Book page 59

Ask students to think about the items in the pictures they are familiar with. Ask, *Do you share food with your friends? Why?* And tell them to talk to a classmate about it. Then invite pairs to share the words with the whole class.

Draw food you like for your party.

Materials and preparation
- Crayons or colored pencils
- Project Book page 59
- Sheets of paper

Have students draw their favorite food for their own parties. They tell the class about the party food they drew. Prompt them to say *I like ice cream and cake*, for example.

DIFFERENTIATED INSTRUCTION

BELOW LEVEL
Retell the story.

Have students retell the story in groups, after having practiced all together

ABOVE LEVEL

Have students work in groups to share their drawings and talk about the food they like and dislike. They should talk about their own likes and dislikes, as well as others classmates' preferences.

CLOSING

Play a party game. Sing the *Happy birthday song*.

Materials and preparation
- Balloons
- Masking tape
- Puppet

Tell students that it is the puppet's birthday today. Say, *It is the puppet's birthday today. Let's sing Happy birthday.* Sing and have students sing along. Tell students that they will play a birthday party game. Place students in three lines, one behind the other. Ask the first ones on the line to place their balloons between their legs. Say, *Go* and have students jump to the finish line. If the balloon is lost or if it pops, they are out. If it doesn't, they go to the end of the line and wait for their next turn. Have students say *happy birthday* and *goodbye* to the puppet. Have the puppet say *thanks* and *goodbye* to the students.

Unit 8 What do you like about school?

Learning goals
- Talk about what boys and girls like to play with
- Understand that it is OK for boys and girls to play together with all kinds of toys
- Talk about a favorite toy

Main language content
Do you like playing with cars?
Toys: *car, dinosaur, doll, teddy bear, train, tricycle*

OPENING

Circle time

Materials and preparation
- Puppet
- Visual schedule pictures

Have all the students sit in a circle, facing you. Review the procedures for gathering in a circle. Say *hello* to them and invite them to greet you back.
Place the visual schedule pictures face down in the circle. Say the schedule for the day, one activity at a time, and have different students turn over the cards looking for the picture that represents the activity.

> **Note to teachers**
>
> The next four lessons work with the way students relate to their classmates and friends, toys, and school materials. Make sure students understand that they are all different and relate to each other in different ways, but they should respect each other as classmates and play and share their things with everyone.

Tongue twister

Materials and preparation
- Toy phone (or make one using craft paper)

Bring out the toy phone and tell students you are going to teach them a very short and popular tongue twister.
I scream, you scream, we all scream for ice cream!
Have students repeat the tongue twister several times and then give the toy phone to one of them. Tell them to pretend they are talking to someone on the phone and say the tongue twister as fast as possible. Then have them pass on the toy phone to another student who has to do the same really fast!

Personal, Social, and Emotional Development

ACTIVE LEARNING

Listen. Match the toys with the children.

Materials and preparation
- Audio library - class content
- Project Book page 61

Help students open their Project Book to page 61. Elicit the names of the toys from students. Tell students they are going to listen to two children talking about what they like to play with and they will match the children and the toys. Say, *The boy's name is Mike and the girl is Kelly. Let's see what they like. They sometimes play together.* Play the audio (track 08) and pause after each line for students to match.

> ### Audio script
>
> **Mike:** *I love teddy bears. I like dinosaurs and cars, too.*
> **Kelly:** *I like dolls, but I like cars, too. I play with Mike.*

Draw yoursef with your favorite toy.

Materials and preparation
- Crayons or colored pencils
- Project Book page 61

Draw students' attention to the next activity and ask them to draw themselves with a favorite toy. Invite them to tell their classmates about it.

Play *Musical toys.*

Materials and preparation
- Audio library - songs
- Several toys such as teddy bear, toy car, train

Have students sit in a circle and place the toys in the middle. Explain that you are going to play some music and when it stops you will ask them to touch one of the toys.
Play the music, then stop and shout, *Touch the train!* Students then have to touch the train.

DIFFERENTIATED INSTRUCTION

BELOW LEVEL

Materials and preparation
- Project Book page 61

Match the toys to the children in groups or pairs.

ABOVE LEVEL

Ask students to describe the children and the toys in the pictures (colors, shapes, etc.)

CLOSING

Toy gallery

Materials and preparation
- Students' drawings of a favorite toy

Display students' drawings of a favorite toy around the classroom. Ask students to go around, point to drawings, and talk about what they see. *He is playing with a doll. She likes dinosaurs.*, etc. Check if they can identify whose drawing it is.

Say goodbye.

Have students tell you goodbye with their body language. Remind them to be very creative and say the word *goodbye* or *bye* as they do it.

LISTEN. FIND MATT, ALLIE, SAM, AND OLIVE.

DRAW YOURSELF IN THE SANDBOX.

PERSONAL, SOCIAL, AND EMOTIONAL DEVELOPMENT • WHAT DO YOU LIKE ABOUT SCHOOL? • UNIT 8 63

Learning goals
- Learn about playing together and being a good classmate
- Say where things are at school
- Describe themselves

Main language content
My book is on the chair. He is blond.
He has red shorts.
Prepositions: *in, on, under*
School: *board, book, chair, crayon, glue (stick), notebook, pen, pencil sandbox, table*

OPENING

Circle time

Materials and preparation
- Puppet
- Visual schedule pictures

Have all the students sit in a circle, facing you. Review the procedures for gathering in a circle. Say *hello* to them and invite them to greet you back.
Place the visual schedule pictures face down in the circle. Say the schedule for the day, one activity at a time, and have different students turn over the cards looking for the picture that represents the activity.

Naughty ghost!

Move the classroom material before students' arrival. Make sure you move things around in a way that students can use the three prepositions *in, on, under* and classroom vocabulary. For example, place books under a student´s chair, a pencil on the table, crayons in a notebook, etc.
When students come in explain to them that last night a naughty little ghost came inside the classroom and moved things around. Students have to go around, find the things in unusual places, point to them and say, *The book is under the chair*.

Personal, Social, and Emotional Development

ACTIVE LEARNING

Listen. Find Matt, Allie, Sam, and Olive.

Materials and preparation

- Audio library - class content
- Project Book page 63

Help students open their Project Book to page 63. Ask them, *What can you see in the picture?* Elicit the words *boy, girl, sandbox, toys*.
Now tell students you are going to read the descriptions of these children and they have to listen carefully. Once they understand who you are describing they can point to the child. Read each description once. Then play the audio (track 09) and pause after each sentence.

Audio script

He is a boy. He has blond hair. He has yellow shorts and a red T-shirt. His name is Matt.
She is a girl. She has brown hair. She has blue shorts and a green T-shirt. Her name is Olive.
He is a boy. He has red hair. He has purple shorts and a black T-shirt. His name is Sam.
She is a girl. She has black hair. She has pink shorts and an orange T-shirt. Her name is Allie.

Draw yourself in the sandbox.

Materials and preparation

- Crayons
- Project Book page 63

When all students have identified each of the children, ask them to draw themselves in the sandbox.

Show and tell.

Materials and preparation

- Ask students to bring an item from home that helps others get to know them better (a favorite mug, pajamas, etc.)

Have students present their item and talk about how special it is for them and how it helps others get to know them better. This activity has the purpose to connect the student's personal life at home with the student's life at school.

DIFFERENTIATED INSTRUCTION

BELOW LEVEL

Materials and preparation

- Audio library - class content
- Project Book page 63

Read the description of the children in the sandbox and pause after each sentence making sure students are pointing to what they have heard. For example, when they hear *He is a boy*, students point to a boy.

ABOVE LEVEL

Ask students to describe the children on page 63. They can do this in pairs or in groups.

CLOSING

Describe your classmate. Say goodbye.

Ask a student to come forward and have their classmates describe them. Students can describe their hair, clothes, etc. When students have finished ask them if they are similar to their classmate and how.
Ask students to shake hands or hug each other to say *goodbye*. Then shake hands with each one of them and elicit *bye*.

OPENING

Circle time

Materials and preparation
- Puppet
- Visual schedule pictures

Say *hello* to students and have them greet you back. Encourage them to greet the puppet, too.
Review the attention getter: *Beep, beep, honk, honk*. When you say *beep, beep*, students respond *honk, honk*.
Bring the visual schedule pictures and place them in the circle. Ask a volunteer to help you get the pictures as you read the schedule for the day.

Decorate your tube.

Materials and preparation
- Crayons
- Fine marker pens
- TP roll tubes

Hand out a TP roll tube to each student. Give them a selection of crayons or fine marker pens. Have students decorate their tubes any way they want. Explain that they are making a personal counter for the game they are going to play.

Learning goals
- Follow instructions in a game
- Recognize written numbers up to nine
- Count to ten

Main language content

My counter is (blue and red).
Numbers: *1-10*
School: *board, book, eraser, notebook, playground, ruler, teacher*
Colors: *blue, green, orange, pink, purple, red, yellow*

ACTIVE LEARNING

Talk about your counter.

Materials and preparation

- Students' counters

Have students work in small groups and talk about their counter. Encourage them to say what color it is and talk about any pictures they have drawn on it.

> **Note to teachers**
>
> When working in groups, it is important to tell students to listen to their classmates while they are speaking. Remind them that everyone has a turn to listen and to speak.

Listen and move your counter. Say the number and the word.

Materials and preparation

- Project Book page 65
- Students' counters

Help students open their Project Book to page 65. Explain that they are going to play the game in pairs. Tell students the rules of the game: They listen to their classmate, who will say a number from one to nine, and move to that number. They will repeat the number and say what is in that picture. If they can't say the word, their classmate can help.
Remind students to take turns saying numbers and moving counters. Monitor and help as needed.

Think! question

Materials and preparation

- Project Book page 65

Ask students to think about the number of words they know that are in the pictures. Ask, *How many words do you know?* And tell them to talk to a classmate about it. Then invite pairs to share the words with the whole class.

DIFFERENTIATED INSTRUCTION

BELOW LEVEL
What object is this?

Materials and preparation

- A box
- Blindfold (optional)
- Classroom objects: *book, crayon, eraser, pencil, sharpener*

Put some classroom objects in a box and explain to students that they will have to find out what the object is only by touching it.
Have another student say what the object really is. You can blindfold the student or ask them to close their eyes.

ABOVE LEVEL

Have everyone sit down in a circle. One by one, ask students to stand up and pick a classroom object. Have them show this object and call on a classmate to say what it is.

CLOSING

Sing the *Goodbye song*.

Materials and preparation

- Audio library - songs
- Puppet

Gather students in a circle. Have them sing the *Goodbye song* (track 05).
Sing and pause it. Ask students a question about game rules. Suggestions:
Can we follow rules? (Yes)
Can we play alone? (No)
Can we get angry when we lose? (No)
Continue the song and pause it a few more times.
Then play the whole song and have students sing and dance while waving goodbye to you and the puppet.

ARE THE CHILDREN BEING NICE TO EACH OTHER? COLOR.

THINK! HOW CAN YOU BE NICE TO SOMEONE TODAY?

PERSONAL, SOCIAL, AND EMOTIONAL DEVELOPMENT • WHAT DO YOU LIKE ABOUT SCHOOL? • UNIT 8 • 67

Learning goals
- Respect others and each other's turn
- Identify and name playground equipment

Main language content
Your turn!
Push me, please.
I'll help you!
Thank you!
Playground equipment: *slide, swing, monkey bars, trampoline*
Shapes: *circle, rectangle, square, triangle*

OPENING

Circle time

Materials and preparation
- Puppet
- Visual schedule pictures

Say *hello* to students and have them greet you back. Encourage them to greet the puppet, too. Ask how they are and help them answer with the words they know.
Bring the visual schedule pictures and place them in the circle. Ask a volunteer to help you get the pictures as you read the schedule for the day.

Listen and jump.

Materials and preparation
- Masking tape
- Large shapes cutouts of colored construction paper (square, circle, rectangle, triangle)

Stick the large shapes on the floor. Have students line up, one after the other. Call out the different shapes one at a time to the first student in line, e.g., *Circle!* The student should jump onto the shape you call out. Make sure that all students have a go, and that all of them jump onto every shape. Call out the shapes in random order.

Personal, Social, and Emotional Development

ACTIVE LEARNING

Are the children being nice to each other? Color.

Materials and preparation
- Pictures: a slide, a swing, a trampoline, and monkey bars (if available at the school playground, take pictures of them)
- Project Book page 67

Help students open their Project Book to page 67 and ask them what is happening in the picture. Elicit as many words as possible from them. Hold up the pictures one at a time and teach students the new words. Point to the first picture. Ask students what they can see. Ask them what they think the child is saying. Take their ideas and then teach them: *Your turn!* Have students practice the phrase chorally and individually. Continue with the other pictures, teaching the nice and respectful things the children are saying.

Second picture Boy: *Push me, please.*
Third picture Boy 1: *I'm scared!*
Third picture Boy 2: *You're fine. I'll help you!*
Fourth picture Girl 1: *Where are my shoes?*
Fourth picture Girl 2: *Here!*
Fourth picture Girl 1: *Thank you!*

Ask, *Are the children being nice?* Then tell students to color the slide, the swings, the monkey bars, and the trampoline. When they are ready, ask them what their favorite piece of playground equipment is.

> **Note to teachers**
> If possible, take students to the playground and have them point and name the equipment they see there. Allow them sometime to play and encourage them to use the phrases they learned (*Your turn, Please, Push me,* etc.). Finally, gather the students together and ask each one what equipment they played on.

Think! question

Materials and preparation
- Project Book page 67

Ask students the *Think!* question: *How can you be nice to someone today?* And tell them to talk to a classmate about it. Then invite pairs to share the words with the whole class.

Act it out.

Invite a couple of students to the front. Tell them to pretend they are playing on the playground. Have the other students guess the equipment they are playing on.

DIFFERENTIATED INSTRUCTION

BELOW LEVEL
Answer the questions

Materials and preparation
- Project Book page 67

Go through the pictures again, asking questions about what the children are doing and what they are saying. Remind them to raise their hand before answering the question and respect their classmates' turn. When students get to the right answer, have them all clap twice.

ABOVE LEVEL

Have students act out the dialogues in pairs. First see if they can remember the dialogues. If not, help them remember. Work with each pair individually or separate those who remember the dialogue from those who don't to help them in different ways.

CLOSING

Burst the balloon. Sing the *Goodbye song*.

Materials and preparation
- Audio library - songs
- Balloon
- Puppet

Have everyone stand in a circle. Give the puppet the balloon and say, *You have the balloon. It's your turn to speak. What's your favorite part of today's class?* Have the puppet answer, *I like (the book).* Then have the puppet throw the balloon to a student, who will have their turn answering the question. Remind students to listen as it is their classmate's turn to speak. Repeat until everyone has had a chance to speak. Then sing the *Goodbye song* (track 05) and say *goodbye* to students.

Notes

Notes

Notes

Notes

Notes

Notes

Notes

Notes

Notes